on track ...

Deep Purple

from 1984

every album, every song

Phil Kafcaloudes

sonicbondpublishing.com

Sonicbond Publishing Limited
www.sonicbondpublishing.co.uk
Email: info@sonicbondpublishing.co.uk

First Published in the United Kingdom 2025
First Published in the United States 2025

British Library Cataloguing in Publication Data:
A Catalogue record for this book is available from the British Library

ISBN 978-1-78952-354-6

Typeset in ITC Garamond & ITC Avant Garde
Printed and bound in England

Graphic design and typesetting: Full Moon Media

on track ...

Deep Purple

from 1984

every album, every song

Phil Kafcaloudes

sonicbondpublishing.com

Acknowledgements

Jackie, for sharing her musical knowledge throughout this project. Peter Hurley and Mick Collopy, for their classical and piano insights. The time-generous Joe Lynn Turner, Steve Morse, Glenn Hughes, and the men who travelled on so much of DP's journey, Colin Hart and Drew Thompson. And to the late Jon Lord: thank you for always being a gentleman and giving me the privilege to talk with you.

on track ...

Deep Purple

from 1984

Contents

Introduction

In 2024, Deep Purple celebrated the 40th anniversary of their reunion by releasing their 23rd album, *=1,* with recently recruited guitarist Simon McBride.

McBride's addition made this just the latest of many versions of DP since its original 1968 inception. Fans had watched new members pass through the world of DP and saw how these personnel changes inevitably brought different musical styles. As well as the hard rock of its most famous lineup (the 1969-1973 Mk II with Ritchie Blackmore, Ian Gillan, Roger Glover, Jon Lord and Ian Paice), the band would flirt with progressive rock, orchestral music, jazz, funk, blues and even country.

And this variation in team and style was exactly what the group was originally supposed to be about. When the former Searchers drummer Chris Curtis got together with Lord and Blackmore in 1967, their band was to be called Roundabout and it was supposed to operate just like that carnival ride with musicians jumping on and off, each bringing something different to their predecessor.

Curtis disappeared before a track was laid down, but his vision remained in Blackmore's mind, and he became the driver of changes over the first seven years, starting with the disposal of originating singer Rod Evans and bassist Nick Simper in 1969 for Gillan and Glover, who were themselves replaced by David Coverdale and Glenn Hughes four years later. Eventually, ironically, tensions over evolving styles saw Blackmore himself pull out in 1975 after disparaging Coverdale and Hughes's funk as 'shoeshine music'. This left only two original members, Lord and Paice. Blackmore's replacement, Tommy Bolin, stayed for one album, but as loved as he was by the rest of the band, he was less suited to the rigours of touring and the unfavourable reactions from the Blackmore fans in the audience.

The band finally pulled the pin after one particularly unfortunate concert in 1976, and for the next eight years, there was no DP. Coverdale went on to create Whitesnake, offering places to Paice and Lord with the understanding it was Coverdale who was the boss this time. Roger Glover was to join up with Blackmore's Rainbow, and Gillan was finding his own successes and stresses with his businesses, self-titled bands, and Black Sabbath.

When the word got around to the former DP Mk II members in 1983 that a reunion was being proposed, there was some confusion. Lord remembers a surprised Gillan telling him that Blackmore would never go for it. Lord responded that it was the guitarist's idea. But in the strange way of DP's historical memory, Blackmore told Jerry Bloom in 1995 that the originator was Gillan himself:

> Gillan came along and talked us into it. I did it basically because it was easy money. The money was dangled in front of me, and I thought: 'Well, the Rainbow thing's going well, but shit, okay.' I thought we'd do maybe one LP.

Blackmore may have felt this way, but Gillan told the New York press in October 1984 that the reunion was not going to be 'a one-off, one album, one tour. It can be a rock n' roll lifetime.'

And so it has proved, although more faces have changed over the years, because not even maturity and financial incentives could stop old fractures from reappearing. These led to the vaudeville of Blackmore dropping a plate of spaghetti on Gillan's head backstage after a concert. Then there was the turmoil of the sacking and reinstatement of Gillan, the eventual exit of Blackmore, and his replacement by Joe Satriani and then former Dixie Dreg, Steve Morse. This was followed by Lord's departure in February 2002, which led to the recruitment of the former Rainbow keyboardist Don Airey. This last change completed DP's most stable lineup, which recorded and toured together for almost 20 years before Morse was replaced by Simon McBride.

This book tells this sometimes bizarre post-reunion story through their music and, to an extent, their touring. Neither was always completely successful, as the band seemed to be either searching for synergy in their sound or for a commercially successful product that did not sacrifice artistic integrity. Gillan and Glover's lyrics are especially valuable to the story because, apart from the band's internecine battles, we also see other clues in those words, things like the hardship of the road and insights into Gillan's own growing frustrations with a society that he was despairing of as too woke, too violent, too ridiculous.

The band's recent chart success has proved the reunion was worth the bother. The band has not just resurfaced but written a new story for a new audience. Gillan would thrill to tell interviewers how his 17-year-old daughter told him her friends considered DP cool. Just like any other musician, Gillan revered relevance.

All these things make this latter phase of DP an interesting study, not just of a successful band loved by so many but also of the musicians behind the songs who just wanted to play their music and sometimes found it was not as simple as that.

Note: I have featured only those live recordings (in order of concert date, not release date) that were either contractual (*Nobody's Perfect*), important to the band's story (*Come Hell Or High Water* and *Concerto For Group And Orchestra 1999*) or showed the band after a change of lineup (e.g. *Live At The Olympia 1996*). I also include *Live At The NEC* because it is Jon Lord's handover to Airey, and so it is in itself a band event.

During the reunion years, there have been reissues and remixes of the 1960s and 1970s albums. They have not been included because this book focuses on the band's post-reunion work.

Perfect Strangers (1984)

Personnel
Ian Gillan: vocals
Richie Blackmore: guitars
Jon Lord: keyboards
Roger Glover: bass, synthesizer
Ian Paice: drums and percussion
Record label: Polydor
Recorded at 'Horizons', Stowe, Vermont, US, with Le Mobile Studio between 10 July and 26 August 1984
Produced by Roger Glover & Deep Purple
Release date: 29 October 1984
Highest chart places: UK: 5, US: 17
Running time: 40:02

Album Facts

It would be difficult to differentiate the genesis of *Perfect Strangers* from the facts of the band's reunion. The freshness of some songs tells of the players' joy in the revival, although getting to this point was not simple. These five musicians had not played as a group for 11 years and were no longer the hippy musicians of the early 1970s. They were now five middle-aged family men who really had nothing to prove. They still retained the musical hunger, but it was a new kind of hunger without financial urgency (although none of them were necessarily rich, the residuals from their five-way song credits from all the albums from *In Rock* (1970) through to *Who Do We Think We Are* (1973) continued and continues to provide each with a flow of income).

The reunion started with warmth all around. The video for their January 1985 single 'Perfect Strangers' showed the moment the bandmates reunited in Vermont, with Blackmore playfully feigning a reluctance to shake Gillan's hand before they are all seen laughing as they head out for a game of soccer and a few drinks. Gillan was to tell Greg Prato 35 years later that when the band got into the studio, things did not go as smoothly:

> There was a lot of suspicion, worry and nervousness about getting together again. We had a couple of beers, and nobody started playing. Then, Paicey [Ian Paice] started tapping away and people started grooving, and a little shuffle came along. In five minutes, everyone had a smile on their face. So, perfect strangers were how we were before, and perfect strangers are how we are afterwards – with two opposite meanings to the phrase.

One change that would cause discontent down the line was an alteration in writers' credits. When these five musicians worked together in the 1970s, every player received an equal credit and thus an equal royalty split. In 1984,

Blackmore told *Sounds* magazine's Sylvie Simmons that for the reunion, he had dictated a change to 'who writes, gets':

> Writing-wise, it's always been basically three people and it's still those same three people. Sometimes, someone might think they've written something just by turning up to a rehearsal of that particular song.

This meant that Paice and Lord had a writing credit on only one song on this album, but at the time of its release, Lord told the BBC's Tommy Vance that he had no frustration at this because Blackmore had most of the ideas:

> I got to Vermont with... you know, bits and pieces. Ragtag and bobtail stuff that I'd had trundling around the back corridors of my head, things that I thought might be useful. Ritchie arrived, bursting at the seams with fabulous stuff! I just threw what I had away.

Then came the question of who was to produce the album. Glover told Vance that without making a conscious decision, he found himself once again in the producer's chair:

> I could not stay out of the control room. So, by kind of unspoken consent, I became the producer. But having done it, I felt really good about it.

Tour manager Colin Hart told the author Glover worked hard at the role, being the first one in every morning for *Perfect Strangers* and the last one out at night, and his producing experience with Rainbow, Michael Schenker, Nazareth and Judas Priest meant this album was always going to be a step forward in production terms from earlier DP product.

The resulting album achieved good chart success (platinum selling and going to number five in the UK, two in Germany and the edge of the *Billboard* top ten in the US), but creatively it is a mixed bag. It is difficult to put one's finger on what is missing. Every song is executed well by all players; the instruments are mixed to a distinctness and there are certainly some of the canon's most standout songs. Yet there is sometimes a distance between band and listener. Maybe it's because *Perfect Strangers* shouts at times, trying a smidgeon too hard. There's also its schizoid nature. It is a mix of progressive and tough rock, and unlike some of their 1970s albums, the two don't always sit well with each other. Thirty years later, Roger Glover told *Classic Rock*'s Paul Rees that the album was 'not quite hanging together'. Listening to the set straight through, it's hard to disagree.

Live, it was a different story. On the Australian leg of their tour, the band jammed and frolicked; even the normally reticent Blackmore danced around the stage. In the Sydney show on 14 December, he went on all fours and playfully grabbed a surprised Gillan around the legs. During the same show

Gillan took part (on the congas) on a Rainbow song. The goodwill amongst the band members continued on the world tour to support the album, including headlining to more than 70,000 people at Knebworth. It was looking good for band harmony. For now.

Album Cover

A minimalist but effective cover to herald in a new era. The front has a high-contrast image of the new DP logo in the centre of an almost-black background. The logo sparkles as if to make the point that this is a new band (which, of course, it's not) for a new era (which it was hoping to be). While the band's name is printed across the top, it is the embossed-look logo that stands out. The album name is less visible, being smaller and in red at the bottom, and in non-reader-friendly calligraphy. Overall, it's a sharp front that, notably, avoids pictures of the band. That is left for the back cover, where the members are shown looking ready for business, and if there was any concern about the decade since their last DP outing together, they have been monochromed and posterised into a less ageing blue and white. Under them is a track listing, production credits and copyright information. Inside, the gatefold is rather more revelatory. Here, we see the band mooning about with their technicians and roadies, and shots of soccer games, beer-swilling, picnicking with locals and, only occasionally, playing a musical instrument. It all looks like a great time was being had. You would never imagine this kind of collage on a Whitesnake or Rainbow album, and this reveals the marketing of the reunion group: they are old friends, happy to be together. And at that time, they probably were. The lyrics and production credits are on the left of both gatefold pages.

All tracks by Blackmore, Gillan and Glover (unless otherwise noted)

'Knocking At Your Back Door'

A layered and ominous organ opening heralds the revamped DP. Simple, solid bass and drums join in, and Lord goes into a syncopated *Jaws*-like motif. Blackmore enters next, introducing himself with a riff that is as solid as Lord's while being a huge hard rock contrast to it. Gillan comes in last and brings with him a lyric about snobbish and uptight women oral-sexed back into life, an odd contrast to the complexity and promise of the instruments. It's an effective melody and a lyric of smarts with double entendres galore, but it feels like it belongs to a different backing. Phrases like 'a common cunning linguist' may work on first hearing, but they were never destined to be stayers (perhaps Gubbins had spent too much of his long DP off-season listening to Bon Scott?) The lyric bears even less correlation to its music video, which depicts a post-apocalyptic world with the wreckage of human life, burning buildings, buried musical instruments and feral humans who look like extras from a *Mad Max* film encountering helmeted soldiers. All this as Gillan sings about chasing girls. Baffling in every way.

For all this, it's a song that is achingly close to being a classic. If only.

'Under The Gun'

Now we move to the straight rock that revisits the four-to-the-floor of 'Hard Lovin' Man' from *In Rock*. Blackmore told the BBC's Tommy Vance at the time that this was his best work on the album. Considering he was never a fan of AC/DC, it's odd that his strumming has quite some resemblance to Malcolm Young's exuberant work on 'If You Want Blood, You Got It'. The difference here is that Lord cleverly finishes Blackmore's riff, so it's not just a guitar thing. The whole band shares this enthusiasm, giving a feel of a band finding its mojo again. It's certainly strong, with the first guitar solo melding into a short Rainbow-like interlude before the rest of the band comes back sharp as a knife. On many of the fast rock songs on this album, Lord can hardly be heard, but not so here, where he equals the guitar. Gillan's lyrics gravitate between extremely clever to the terribly obvious as they take us back to the 'Child In Time' theme of the futility of war and how the innocents are the ones who suffer. It's a theme he would return to in later years, especially when the internecine band battles heat up.

'Nobody's Home' (Blackmore, Gillan, Glover, Lord, Paice)

A strange one, this. Although it is the only song on the album credited to all five band members, this is dominated by Gillan's aggressive lyrics, which mirror, and take further, his acid commentary on 'Smooth Dancer' from his last DP album, *Who Do We Think We Are*. The target in that song was Blackmore. In this case, the lyrical clues would suggest the same here, particularly the references to the subject being a king (hence male) and his image (a rock star?), but given the degree of goodwill professed by everyone involved (Gillan himself later saying the recording sessions were 'wrapped up in warmth, care and love'), it would be a surprise if Gillan let the attack dogs loose at his bandmate so early. In three years, maybe. And, given Gillan's low view of various band management over the years, the song could be simply his treatise on incompetence. Musically, this is a straight rocker (after some Lord noodling at the start) with an edge of cowbell, making this a tough, angry song that showcases the band's cohesion.

'Mean Streak'

Another mid-fast track, this time with a hard boogie shuffle feel. Unlike 'Nobody's Home', the chorus is the centrepiece and an earworm of sorts. Glover's bass shows some inventive flourishes, playing octaves of E throughout and on the guitar solo. Unfortunately, the song fades as things get interesting, with Lord just starting to get seriously involved. Perhaps it was a time constraint because the song ends side one of the vinyl album and the centre label was looming. Whatever the reason, this is not one of the set's best. Gillan's terrific voice, slightly risqué lyric and the bouncing guitar riff are the only things that keep this from being a filler track.

'Perfect Strangers'

A highlight of the album and one that Gillan, to this day, calls majestic. As with the opening track, this showcases Lord, with Blackmore taking a rare back seat. Lord seems to have taken note of John Paul Jones's anthemic synths that were used so much on Led Zeppelin's *In Through The Out Door* and infuses this track with an organ splendour that is so embedded in the rhythm that it doesn't have a solo-spot feel.

Blackmore is still in the mix, mirroring the synth work and delivering nicely timed injections and rises, and one can hear his fingers sliding up strings in a couple of places.

It all melds with Gillan's lyrics, which are clever and speak to the moment (the brittle reunion). These are witty words from a man who understands just what he's getting himself into. A lovely moment comes with the descending sequence as he sings: 'You know I must remain inside this silent well of sorrow'. Was he, perhaps, the only one to see where this was all going to go in a few albums' time?

Cryptic lyrics aside, it is a song that proves that if you slow it all down a bit and give space, these guys will know exactly how to fill it. Paice does a Ringo very well here, choosing not to showcase himself and only injecting fills when there's a need to force the listener through to the next sequence. Unlike on most of the album, there is no Blackmore solo. It isn't needed. There is plenty of space given to the 9/4 section towards the end, and this bookends the piece perfectly. In May 2024, Glover revealed to *Classic Rock*'s Dave Ling that Blackmore had tried out the song with Rainbow several years before but could not get it working, but the DP lyrics gave it the finishing touch:

> Ian and I used bits and pieces of poetry to write those lyrics. We had an idea about a soul being reborn and being trapped in a new body. The other person knows you're there, but they can't do anything about it. It sounds strange, but it is strange. It was only when the song was finished that we realised it is about Deep Purple.

The original idea for the song may have come from Blackmore, with lyrics solely by Gillan and Glover, but It is still one of the great oddities of the DP catalogue that Lord gets no writing credit for a song in which he dominates so much.

This album may not be every Purple fan's favourite and it's not even all the band members' favourite, but this title track, along with 'Hungry Daze' shows what the new Deep Purple could've been if they had chosen a more progressive route in this rebirth. Magnificent.

'A Gypsy's Kiss'

A rare bass opening fashions into a fast rush with Lord leading the riffing. The first guitar break, which comes ever so close to collapsing right at its end, is saved by a transition into a tight, classically inspired double solo by Lord, which has tones of his work on 'Burn'. Under all this is Paice, who is muscular, with his bass drum playing double time and never flagging for a moment. Despite all the great work, it seems, like the guitar solo, to be on the edge of falling into a heap, saved only by a quick fade. Nevertheless, Gillan belts out snappy lyrics that cite John Wayne and the Alamo, revealing his fascination with American cowboy westerns. And it's great to hear his cheeky laugh once again. 'We can rock n' roll' sings Gillan. You bet.

'Wasted Sunsets'

The power ballad done DP-style. It's big, with strong guitar motifs, and Gillan sings this song of regret as though he is as angry as disappointed. Blackmore's two solos are masterworks of quick fingering that have the same intensity as the vocal. However, never has so much work been put into a song that just doesn't deliver emotionally. Still, this was the 1980s, and in the 1980s, there were certain things groups felt they had to do, the power ballad being one of them. They would not try another one until Joe Lynn Turner seven years later. The pace, though, is a clever contrast to what was to follow.

'Hungry Daze'

The album proper ends with the third of its progressive songs. It starts with a tight machine gun intro that highlights a synergy between Lord, Paice, and Blackmore. The lyrics are equally as clever. Telling of the band's first incarnation from its 'dark and sweaty' first rehearsal through to a cute reference to the making of *Machine Head*, this is an evocation of those high-volume times, with a nod to the girls who came on the journey. A contrasting middle layers staccato keyboards and guitar before Gillan returns to finish the song and album in the present, about the reunion band still being loud and hungry with the bad times left way behind. Gillan sings from the heart on this, perhaps more than on any other track on this comeback album. This, and the mid-song drums, emotive guitar solo and keyboard breaks (although again, Lord gets no writing credit), make this almost as majestic as 'Perfect Strangers' and the most apt closer one could imagine for this album.

'Not Responsible' (Cassette and CD bonus track)

Another high-energy tune that probably missed out on the original LP listing because of its similarity in tempo and punch to some of the other songs, despite flitting between some extraordinary tempo changes and having one of the most tasteful slow guitar solos of the album sessions. Gillan sings with commitment about a footloose man justifying his lifestyle, although the lyrics could have been so much more, particularly with the repeated titular refrain.

It's just that those lyrics skim with a bit too much shallowness. Power drums, power chords and the first 'fuck' in the DP canon betray a band trying to keep up with its metal competition, something DP had never done before.

'Son Of Alerik' (Blackmore) (1999 CD bonus track)

In recent years, Glover and Gillan have described DP as a jamming band, and this bonus track shows the band in that process. This Blackmore song is a slow blues that might well have been recorded just as the members picked up their instruments. There's nothing demanding nor particularly inspired, with each member noodling around, throwing in whatever they feel like. With a 'When A Blind Man Cries' type of lyrics, this could have been something affecting. As it is, particularly running at over ten minutes, it's easy to see why it never made the album cut or even the original CD as a bonus.

Perfect Strangers Live 1984 (2013)

Personnel
Ian Gillan: vocals
Richie Blackmore: guitars
Jon Lord: keyboards
Roger Glover: bass
Ian Paice: drums and percussion
Record label: Eagle Vision
Recorded at Melbourne Sports & Entertainment Centre, Australia, on 18 December 1984
Produced by Roger Glover/Deep Purple
Release date: 11 October 2013
Highest chart places: Germany: 20, Austria: 53
Running time: 100.00

Album Facts

In November 1984, only six months after the announcement of the reunion, the Mk II band was in New Zealand for the start of its first tour in 11 years before moving to Perth in Western Australia, then Sydney and Melbourne.

This album, released 30 years after its recording, documents this live DP rebirth and does it in a grand way as a double CD and a DVD video album, making this a visual as well as an aural document of the band performing early in the reunion.

Tour manager Colin Hart told the author that touring in 1984 was much bigger than it had been in 1973, and Lord told *Kerrang*'s Geoff Barton he insisted on some touring changes:

> In 1972, we were on the road non-stop for 44 weeks. I never want to have to experience that kind of pressure again. I remember saying, 'OK, if we do it, let's do one thing, let's make sure that we take our time. Let's do a gig and have a day off. Even if it becomes a financially insecure exercise, fuck it, let's do it that way'.

Clearly, the lesson was not learned because, despite Lord's insistence on time off, the tour got increasingly booked up, repeating the same burnout risk as before. One can see how this happened. Ticket sales were so big that DP would become the second-highest-grossing touring act in the US that year. Hart told the author that it got to the stage where Gillan and Lord started bucking against the load. But early on, when this set was recorded, things were handled more generously to the band, with shows staggered with (mostly) on and off days.

The material on this set was all recorded at a single concert at the Melbourne Sports & Entertainment Centre, which had been the swimming arena for the 1956 Melbourne Olympic Games. The concert had just followed a huge selling three days in Sydney, during which former Beatle George Harrison had joined them onstage for a version of Little Richard's *Lucille*. The author was at that concert and remembers Gillan introducing Harrison as 'Arnold from Liverpool' to an audience who seemed to take a while to recognise the ex-Beatle. Harrison later told Jonathan Graham that the decision to appear was so impromptu that he was 'playing the wrong key, but it didn't seem to matter.' Such was the bonhomie of the times. There was so much of it, in fact, that Blackmore was to tell Dave Ling in 1987 that it was only during this Australian tour that he realised the reunion was going to work.

Although they look fit and are full of energy, Gillan's voice does get tired (Blackmore would later tell Jerry Bloom that Gillan's voice would typically last only about a week on tour), and some songs are played so furiously that band members are often drenched in sweat. And there were moments of tension onstage. On *New, Live & Rare: The Video Collection,* as the band performs 'Black Night' at one of the Sydney concerts, Glover approaches Blackmore, who appears to be having a technical issue, but Blackmore gruffly gestures Glover to get away from him. That bonhomie was obviously already fragile.

Perfect Strangers Live was marginally more successful on release in 1991 than the recording of their concert at Knebworth, which was taped and released early in the reunion (*In The Absence Of Pink, Live At Knebworth 1984)*, charting in both Austria and Germany, but nowhere else.

Album Cover

Although this album was released in 2013, the cover was obviously designed to pay homage to *Perfect Strangers*, with the album name in the red 1984 font. Across the front top is a blue monochrome band image, and under the album and band name is a stage shot of Gillan mid-prance with a microphone stand as Blackmore appears to be in the middle of soloing. The back cover is equally dark, with another photo that could have been taken either shortly before or after the image on the front. Above a track listing, there is a seven-line liner note by English music journalist Malcolm Dome that heralds the reunion. The booklet starts with a red two-page spread of a stage shot of Gillan on the left and Blackmore on the right, but it's an image that seems more Black Sabbath than DP. The notes in the booklet are full of superlatives, including 'astonishing', 'incredible', 'surreal' and 'another universe'. We know all that.

All tracks by Blackmore, Gillan, Glover, Lord and Paice (unless otherwise noted)

'Highway Star'

Right from this opening number, the band shows that this reunion is about unfinished business. They show the same energy they had back in the early

1970s and then some. The song is faster than the original, and they all attack it with a busyness that might be a bit too much for the song but is a statement of intent, right from Glover's eighth-note bass line and Paice's uncharacteristic showmanship, flailing his arms in a way more Keith Moon than Ian Paice. Gillan, in tight leather pants and a shirtless vest, is having a great time while having trouble getting every word out at this higher tempo. Gillan sings along with Blackmore's guitar solo, and Blackmore appears to enjoy the interaction. At several points, Gillan double fists at the Melbourne audience and laughs. Yes, we are back, he could be saying, and no, this is not going to be a pallid greatest hits tour.

'Nobody's Home'
There is no speed ramping on this version of one of their dirtiest new rock songs. Gillan plays with the lyrics a little, making it more aggressive than the recording of only a few months before. Blackmore commands this song though, even using his elbow on the strings. This makes two fiery songs in a row to reintroduce the band to their fans. A mid-tempo number is probably called for now.

'Strange Kind Of Woman'
And it comes in this bluesy hit from 1971. Again, Blackmore offers up very busy solos as though he'd been storing them up. He once again trades lines with Gillan, and there certainly are great moments of camaraderie with Blackmore offering up the 'Jesus Christ Superstar' theme for Gillan (who sang as Jesus on the original 1970 British recording). They laugh together, and then Blackmore goes into 'Waltzing Matilda' and looks to Gillan, who doesn't take the bait this time (perhaps he didn't get the reference or know the words. His shake of the head could suggest either). There is a mistake at the start of the second verse, where Gillan thought they were headed into an instrumental break, but this song is such an example of classic DP improvisation that this was probably never noticed by the screamers in the audience.

'A Gypsy's Kiss' (Blackmore, Gillan, Glover)
Now, things slow right down. Blackmore improvises over some subtle Lord organ work in a 52-second jam. Then, suddenly, this switches into the fast rock of 'A Gypsy's Kiss' led by Lord's wall of keyboards. We are only four songs into the set, but Gillan's voice is starting to sound strained. He tries his best to give the audience his highs, but he either can't get there or thinks better than trying to attempt it. It's no wonder. Despite spacing the dates more than in the 1970s, the tour has already traversed Perth, Adelaide, Auckland, Canberra, Brisbane and three consecutive dates in Sydney before the three nights in Melbourne. A racing number like this seems to be a bridge too far for the singer at this point. It seems Lord had a point with his complaints about crammed touring.

'Perfect Strangers' (Blackmore, Gillan, Glover)
There is some respite in this, the new single. After a short time offstage while Lord goes through his synth introduction, Gillan returns with a fresh voice to deliver what would be one of his better performances in this concert (except for a few coughs and his missing a couple of lines). Overall, it's a solid performance from the band in a song that would become a live staple for the next 40 years.

'Under The Gun' (Blackmore, Gillan, Glover)
The pace ramps up again for this guitar hero track. Blackmore and Glover are in a tight synchronisation, only breaking away from each other in the two guitar solos. The second solo, in particular, is a sterling effort by Blackmore, who slams his guitar on a monitor and finishes crouched on the drum riser. For all these histrionics, he barely misses a note.

'Knocking At Your Back Door' (Blackmore, Gillan, Glover)
The start is note-perfect from the recorded version, if a little more subdued, but this gives Gillan a chance to play with the lyrics. Glover lays down an interesting bass line under the guitar solo, but this can't stop the song from sounding a bit empty. The song trails off with the piping keyboards of the beginning and some soft guitar before a thunderous finale.

'Lazy'
Blackmore fiddles with the intro of this *Machine Head* song, throwing in some staccato notes before racing into a fast take of the opening riff. It's very busy as well as fast, and it's a wonder the band holds it together. The fact it does comes down to the stubbornly tight bass and drum rhythm section. Gillan takes things down a little with his verse and harmonica, but as soon as he finishes, things go into orbit again, with Paice delivering a solo that is heavy on snare and bass drum syncopation and open rolls that turn into crush rolls. This solo dominates the song, taking up more than half of it before Gillan's harmonica closes it out.

'Child In Time'
Clearly a crowd favourite, a gentle Lord opening leads into Gillan, who adds an extra layer of interpretation to his 1970 recorded performance. Gillan scales the highs (if aided by some well-placed echo). Blackmore throws away his recorded solo to vamp into something entirely new that doesn't fit in quite the same way as his work in the studio in 1969, but as a live performance, it still works very well, leaving breaks to allow for the drums and congas to seep through his triplet accents. At around the seven-minute mark, Blackmore wrings his guitar's neck with a freneticism that suits the mayhem inferred by the lyrics. It's wild and angry, but never ever loose. When Blackmore finishes his solo, the band stops with him with precision. It's a

breathtaking moment, and the song is only two-thirds of the way through. If it had finished there, it would have been one of the great recorded live performances, but there is more to come. Gillan's next verse is sung more meaningfully than the first, at times almost spoken, at times scatting, at times almost crying. Then, the highs are hit with beauty. This is a tour de force for all concerned.

'Difficult To Cure' (Ludwig van Beethoven, Blackmore, Glover, Don Airey)
This piece, Blackmore's rock adaptation of Beethoven's 'Ode To Joy', is a big change of pace. Gillan had vetoed songs from the 1973-1976 Coverdale/Hughes version of DP, so it's a wonder that this song, from Blackmore's former band Rainbow, made it on the setlist. When recorded with Rainbow, Glover was the bassist, and the fact that it had no lyrics made it easier to get the nod from Gillan, who just played congas. Obviously, the classicist Lord would have had no objections either. Despite the name, it's not the most difficult piece on the setlist, and was probably just considered a bit of a lark. At four and a half minutes, it was short and sweet and a good lead into Lord's solo.

'Jon Lord Keyboard Solo'
This begins with Lord accompanied only by Glover for a few bars before the bassist leaves the stage to give Lord his six minutes in the spotlight. The Hammond organ is pumped, literally, as Lord rocks the monstrous instrument back and forth. The synthesiser then becomes the focus as he breaks into 'We Wish You A Merry Christmas'. And then, just to mark the fact that many Australians flock to the beach at this time of year, he introduces the theme from the movie *Jaws*. It all sounds spontaneous, but, of course, it isn't, as Paice slides in as Lord starts a New York-style boogie vamp and stops precisely just as Lord goes into Beethoven's 'Für Elise'. Then we go from the sublime to the very silly, with Lord playing between two keyboards in a bit of byplay that could have come from a Keystone Cops silent movie. It all finishes with a sci-fi tone as he tilts the organ over again, this time at a dangerous 40 degrees, in a final gesture to end what was an intriguing trip through his musical encyclopaedia.

'Space Truckin''
After tapping his Hammond in appreciation of its work on the last track, Lord leads into Bach's 'Jesu Joy Of Man's Desiring' which, with the help of Paice's hi-hits, allows the band to come in one at a time until it builds into this, the most playful track on *Machine Head*. It's slightly faster here, but it fits the live mood. Blackmore and Paice do short solos, and it all appears to be heading to an end after four minutes, but it is nowhere near it. There are musical interchanges between Blackmore and Lord, who takes up his soloing as if it

is an interrupted continuation from the previous track. He does a Spanish-style run and then a heavy riff. Both Blackmore and Glover then take it up, slapping their instruments, with Blackmore slamming his Tremolo lever onto the strings. He gets more frantic by the second until it suddenly reverts to the 'Space Truckin" chorus. Much of this is no purpose, but it shows Blackmore in extremis while always being in complete control.

'Black Night'

Once again, the live energy speeds the song and adds a little more of a shuffle to the already shuffling groove. It starts with the same feel as the recorded version, with Blackmore restrained until his solo. The biggest variation from the original single is Gillan's added screams and Blackmore's second solo, some of which is done with one hand.

'Speed King'

This opener from *In Rock* would, in future years, become a plaything for Lord and Blackmore. Not so here in the early days of the reunion. They play the beginning straight, launching into it almost shockingly suddenly. Blackmore's solo appears to slow it all down but doesn't. It is illusory playing at its best. Blackmore dares to introduce the riff from 'Burn' in the middle of his solo, looking cheekily to Lord, who takes him up on it with an answering keyboard. It goes no further, however, with Gillan having vetoed this Coverdale DP song from being done in its entirety. Blackmore and Lord go on to do some silly riff exchanges, including Lord's take on the 'Sailor's Hornpipe' shanty and a simple 'Jingle Bells' before Gillan returns to the stage, and everyone slips back into 'Speed King'. This song may have been recorded in January 1970, but the band play the track with such power that the intervening 15 years years are all but forgotten.

'Smoke On The Water'

Here, at the start of the reunion, they signify that this old hit will remain their anthem for the new era. Gillan starts a tradition, encouraging the audience to sing along as he plays air guitar, interspersed by his calls of 'I can't hear you!'. (He will still not be hearing the audience 40 years later). There is an unusual interlude when Blackmore moves next to Lord and is joined by Glover (so two-thirds of the band are crammed in behind the Hammond). The fun extends to Glover and Blackmore doing some synchronised foot stomping *a la* The Shadows. It all finishes in an extraordinary Gillan wail followed by a very fast jam, which, by Blackmore's look of bemusement, might just be unplanned.

The House Of Blue Light (1987)

Personnel
Ian Gillan: vocals, harmonica
Richie Blackmore: guitars
Jon Lord: keyboards
Roger Glover: bass
Ian Paice: drums and percussion
Record label: Polydor
Recorded at The Playhouse, Stowe, Vermont, US, with Le Mobile Studio between May and June 1986
Produced by Roger Glover/Deep Purple
Release date: 12 January 1987
Highest chart places: UK: 10, US: 34
Running time: 50:38

Album Facts

Bye-bye prog. While *Perfect Strangers* suggested two possible styles for the future, progressive and hard rock, here they surprise by coming up with something else again. There are still moments of full-on rock, but we also have a kind of pop-rock sensibility with plenty of hooks and playful storylines.

The result is an album that doesn't rate particularly highly among fans. Actually, it doesn't rate very highly among the band members, as Blackmore told Jerry Bloom:

> *Perfect Strangers* worked, but the one after that was probably the worst… I've done two really awful LPs: one is *House Of Blue Light.*

It is ironic then that Gillan should say that the album was full of Blackmore's ideas that the others in the band, for the sake of peace, went along with. Gillan admits his unwillingness to do likewise was not understood by his bandmates, and these fissures eventually meant this would be his last full studio album with the band for six years. The lethargy must have affected the other band members, who did the minimum in the studio and left for home. Given this all-round lack of enthusiasm, Roger Glover was left to pull the album together from recordings that were often inadequate or unfinished. He took the tapes to his studio in Greenwich, where, with the help of Gillan, he crafted them into a record.

Its name is a throwback to 1970's *In Rock*'s opening song 'Speed King', which references Little Richard's 'Good Golly Miss Molly' and its line about rockin' at the House of Blue Light. The lines may have been a direct lift, but they got away with it in 1970. Trying their luck, they used the line again and got away with it again.

The wheels might have fallen off before the end of the process, but we have something new on this recording, something quite enjoyable that gave record buyers a tangential DP for their collection. It is a fascinating diversion.

Album Cover

In a neat tie-in with the album name, the front cover is rather beautiful. There's a stately door slightly ajar, with a blue light coming from inside. The package was designed by British couple Davies & Starr, who have also made, among many others, the cover for Robert Plant's *Now & Zen*. The back cover has the five band members' faces from top to bottom, this time not afraid to show their age. Across the back and inside, everything is thrown at it: a child's toy monster, an arrow, a lipstick, a champagne glass and something that could be a dildo. What all this means is anyone's guess. Perhaps it's a joke, like John Lennon and his 'I Am The Walrus' lyric: 'Semolina pilchards climbing up the Eiffel Tower' of which he is supposed to have triumphantly said, 'Let the fuckers work THAT one out.' The same might well have applied here.

All tracks by Blackmore, Gillan and Glover (unless otherwise noted)

'Bad Attitude' (Blackmore, Gillan, Glover, Lord)

The album opens in a menacing tone, with Gillan spitting out a lyric towards someone, perhaps a guitarist, accusing them of having a, yes, bad attitude. He attacks his antagonist with vim:

> You got me locked in a paper cage
> You think I'm chained up but I'm just tied down
> Step aside get out of my way
> I won't hurt you
> I've had enough being pushed around.

Gillan told Mark Putterford that the idea for the title came from a most unlikely place:

> Ritchie [Blackmore] and I were playing football, and we had a row on the pitch, which ended with me telling him to piss off. So he turned around and said, 'There's no need to cop an attitude.'

Despite the subject matter, the band are synchronised. Lord's organ intro is almost church-like, and Paice's drums are again writ large with the booming snare and bass of the times, making it a thrilling, impelling opener. Blackmore delivers two solos joined by a power chord, and Lord ends the song where he starts, with anthemic keyboards. The song would be released as the album's second single, and its video clip is a largely black-and-white affair which focuses heavily on Gillan's face as torn page lines come across the screen. Weird, but fits the angry tone.

'The Unwritten Law' (Blackmore, Gillan, Glover, Paice)
Gillan continues the upbraiding theme with this punitive number that starts as if in the middle of a Blackmore solo. What follows is voice and guitar playing off each other. And that's before the song proper begins. Things slow a little into a Lord pump that has the feel of a shuffle without really shuffling. There is some heavy processing of the drums in the verses, and in a schizoid change, it's all straight rock for the choruses. For the first time in the reunion, Paice gets a kind of showcase, but only at the end and it quickly fades out.

There is no great mystery about those lyrics. There's a bit of flagellation (or self-flagellation) about someone having an affair while on the road. It is a clever dialogue between the transgressor and the transgressed, with the chorus being the victim who has discovered the infidelity. Baffling it is then that Gillan told Mark Putterford in 1987 that this is a song about venereal disease. There are some inspired imageries about 'room within a room, a hole within a hole', but at times, it turns into the incomprehensible:

You've got to learn to take more care
Because if you swim in dirty water
Be careful how you dry your hair

Despite its chastising theme (and the aforementioned disease), this is an uplifting number that again reveals an occasional DP tendency to not quite match the intent of the lyrics with the tone of the music.

'Call Of The Wild' (Blackmore, Gillan, Glover, Lord)
Sheer, sheer fun. This is another mid-tempo track dominated once again by Paice's upfront snare and Lord's keyboard. Despite its exuberant feel, this song is an example of the band's fragmentation because Blackmore is absent for most of the proceedings. In fact, one senses a semi-boycott. It is only at the end that Blackmore plays a short, screaming solo, which quickly fades out, suggesting he didn't stick at it for long. In his place, Lord gets the spotlight with a clever double-layered solo. He may have been filling instrumental holes, but the track is the more interesting for it.

There are no great depths to its story about someone asking a phone operator to find his woman. Gillan goes into a litany of her traits and uses clever contrasts and contradictions:

She got rhythm but no sense of time and
She likes living but she got no friends

Poor operator. This is the most top-40-friendly track on the album, and the band knew it. Released as a single in January 1987, it just scraped into the UK top 100.

The video for the song has as much merrymaking as the song itself. With a Hollywood feel, it shows people attempting (and inevitably failing) to win an audition to perform the song. All manner of dancers and street people, including dwarfs, have a go to the exasperation of the casting agent. What it was trying to say is a mystery, if indeed it was trying to say anything. If it was an attempt to woo the US market, it failed. The single, despite its pop sensibilities, good nature and the group's recent success, did not chart at all stateside. Like that earlier failed attempt to raid the charts ('Never Before' in 1972), this song proved that the band charted best when it wasn't trying to chart.

'Mad Dog'

This track is a huge contrast to the one that precedes it, with an opening power riff from Blackmore pulling the album back into fast rock. Like on most of the album, Gillan delivers vocal gymnastics and cheeky lyrics ('a hard man is good to find') that take us back to the carefree vibe of the 1970s. Lord gets a not particularly demanding solo that goes for all of 20 seconds.

Given the difficulty of the mixing sessions for this album, all these fades reveal where songs were not finished by the time the bandmates dispersed. This is just one of the songs on the album that could have gone further, but alas.

'Black & White' (Blackmore, Gillan, Glover, Lord)

This is Gillan's song. It opens with his harmonica, and he layers his vocal again with an energy that suggests more than the lyrics deliver. It is one of two songs on the album that attack the news media (and probably a few other choice targets like management and contractual obligations). Once again, the music has a verve, but it does seem like an awfully long time since Paice has had anything to do but lay down a bed for everyone else. Gillan's mouth organ, however, has a pretty groovy play-off with the guitar for the last third of the song, which unfortunately turns into a very, very long and entirely unjustified fade-out.

'Hard Lovin' Woman'

It's back to hard, fast 4/4 rock with one of the best guitar riffs on the album. Gillan says this song had no great lyrical significance, with the title only written for a laugh in contrast to the *In Rock* track 'Hard Lovin' Man'. There are other lyrical similarities to that song: a first-person narrative of an anonymous woman who breaks backs in coitus. The difference is that in 1970, Gillan claimed to handle whatever the woman threw at him. Now, 17 years later, it is the woman who has the upper hand:

She chewed me up and spat me out.
She's some woman.

Great guitar aside, this will not rank among a DP classic.

'The Spanish Archer'

The title portends a miserable tone because the Spanish Archer is often taken to mean 'the elbow' or 'getting fired'. And that's what we get: several short and obvious lines where Gillan predicts his inevitable dropping from the band:

Is there someone somewhere waiting in the wings to take my place
Let's not drag it out like a Cagney death scene

Although his autobiography suggests that it was not until well after this time that his employment status came to a head, just why he might feel endangered so soon after the reunion is a mystery. His autobiography refers to resurfacing difficulties with Blackmore, but no more than that. Then again, he could just be singing about the end of a relationship. Whatever the inspiration, he would tell Mark Putterford that he found the song wearing, and it should not have been included on the album.

In many ways, though, this is a classic DP track. Virtuosic wailing guitar solos over a triplet-based drum rhythm give it a real flair. This is one of those tracks where every band member throws everything at it, Glover offering interesting high-note contrasts in the back end of the song. This is a hidden gem that, despite Gillan's misgivings, bears repeated listening.

'Strangeways'

The most experimental song on the album and by far the longest at over seven minutes, it is also Gillan's second foray into social commentary on the set. This time, though, there are no oblique references. It's all obvious: his criticism of media story choice, society's reliance on appearance and religious charlatans. It's also the closest Gillan comes to a dark-night-of-the-soul lyric:

And I say to myself in this academy of fear
Where am I going, what am I doing here

He would later say the song had its origins in his father, who told him that he would understand the nature of life when he grew up. Gillan pushes his voice hard (he would later say this track was his favourite on the album), but the star here is the music, led by Lord with his piping keyboards on the chorus and bridges. Blackmore provides no more than support here with some short lines scattered throughout, sometimes with two or three on top of each other. The most powerful interlude in the song (and probably the whole album) comes at 5.15, where the band rises in unison at a peak that is capped by a screaming guitar that crashes back into the staccato bridge. Now, that's the DP people pay their dosh for. Democratic, brave and new.

'Mitzi Dupree'

After the harmony of the preceding track, we get this strange one. Gillan, in his autobiography, says Blackmore hated this song so much that after hearing the demo, he refused to have anything to do with it. But short of material, Glover and Gillan had to use the demo backing track for the album. It speaks so much about Glover's producing talent that it comes off so clean. That the solo is only a demo also speaks about how Blackmore could produce the goods even when reluctantly noodling.

Being a demo, it is naturally somewhat experimental, with a fascinating confluence of instruments as an opener, followed by a blues in compound time. Lord throws in some honky-tonkish lines, possibly because the band was only in rehearsal mode.

It may have been the words that Blackmore loathed. They are certainly odd. They tell the true story of a woman Gillan met in the first-class section of a plane in the US. This woman was an entertainer who could shoot ping pong balls from a certain orifice, and Gillan developed an infantile crush on her. It's a pretty thin storyline for a song on an album by a major rock act, especially considering the quality of the lyrics elsewhere on the album.

I said what is this queen of the ping pong business
She smiled what do you think
It has no connection with China
I said ooh have another drink

Of course, it's all tongue-in-cheek, but never have vocals of such virtuosity been used in lyrics of so little consequence.

'Dead Or Alive'

And the album ends with a song that traditionally would have the opener: fast, mean and energetic. The song misses the prime spot, most likely because it rarely varies and has the most meagre of hooks. It is saved by a Lord solo that leads into a Blackmore solo and then back to Lord, and then back to Blackmore, etc. In all, they trade places five times. Blackmore gets the closing solo fade out, coming the closest to a classic DP sound, although nowhere near their best. Gillan would say that this, like 'The Spanish Archer', should have been shelved. A closing number is usually an album's strong point. The fact that a track hated by its own writer is put into this position says a lot about the state of the band at the time.

Nobody's Perfect (1988)

Personnel
Ian Gillan: vocals
Richie Blackmore: guitars
Jon Lord: keyboards
Roger Glover: bass
Ian Paice: drums and percussion
Record Label: Polydor
Recorded at Irvine Meadows, US, on 23 May 1987; Phoenix, US, on 30 May; Oslo, Norway on 2 August; Italy (studio unknown) on 6 September; 'Hush' recorded on 26 February 1988
Produced by Roger Glover/Deep Purple
Release date: 5 July 1988
Highest chart places: UK: 38, US: 105
Running time: 88.53

Album Facts

After four years together, DP found itself in a position of having to present a third album to fulfil its obligation to Polydor. Following the malaise of the recording of *The House Of Blue Light,* there wasn't a great deal of enthusiasm about returning to the studio. After much debate, it was agreed that the contract would be fulfilled by a live album, but even then, opinions differed on what kind of live album. Gillan says some members suggested it consist of live *Made In Japan*-era cuts juxtaposed with newly recorded stage material, the aim being to show the band's evolution. In the end, the double album contained only new live material taken from a handful of US and European dates, with the addition of a re-recording of their 1968 US hit, 'Hush', which would be the new single.

Gillan says in his autobiography that the decision to record a live album was odd and that his doubts were proved true when the band listened to the source tapes:

> OK, you can use a studio to make bum notes come out right, but other issues which are more problematic need to be addressed. What happens when the tape runs out in the middle of a song or when there are crackles and screeches? We didn't seem to go into this project with an absolute will to make a great live album. Otherwise, I suppose we'd have taken more than one tape recorder!

Gillan was right. The album is inconsistent. At times, it sounds so tightly compressed that it is as if it was recorded by microphones taping a radio broadcast of the concert; at other times, it booms with the 1980s power rock sound. Gillan often called it an inferior copy of *Made In Japan* and, in a 1994 interview with the Israeli newspaper *Maariv*, was even more pointed:

> I think *Nobody's Perfect* is the most shameful album that we ever released. I can't justify his existence! Over the years, we have made some wonderful albums, but we have also made some to be ashamed of.

The fans agreed. The set may have satisfied a contractual need, but it quelled the momentum generated by the first two reunion albums, missing the US top 100 and just getting into the UK top 40.

So torpid was the background to this album that after a particularly explosive group meeting where a slightly sozzled Gillan belittled the band's management, he was sacked.

Album Cover

This is a clever, if not particularly dynamic, cover from the graphic art design company Hipgnosis (which had designed albums for Led Zeppelin and AC/DC). The cleverness comes from its referencing of DP's earlier work, such as the bubbles drifting down a highway, similar in size to those on *Who Do We Think We Are*. The overall cover is in, of course, shades of deep purple, and it's all heading towards a new dawn (or a sunset). The bubbles have dice markings on them for no obvious reason, and there are scattered images of the Leaning Tower of Pisa, a kettle, a fish that continues across to the back cover, several pencils, a fictional nine-shilling British bank note and finally a tarot card image of a ballet dancer with a beard. The inference is that these (except for the bearded dancer, maybe) are touring items, given that this is a largely live album. Inside the gatefold, we have band photos similar to those on *Perfect Strangers* that give a travelogue of behind-the-scenes moments, including band members in soccer garb, travelling in a plane and clowning in a fake pig's head. Only Lord, Gillan and Blackmore are shown playing an instrument and these all seem to be staged for the camera. Notably, only a few times do two or more band members appear in the same shot. Although there are a few smiles here and there, this spread gives a feel of a band not particularly together. Yes, things were about to escalate.

All tracks by Blackmore, Gillan, Glover, Lord and Paice (unless otherwise noted)

'Highway Star'

It might be a surprise that for an album that is supposed to showcase the reunion DP, the first two tracks both were written in the early 1970s. This opener begins with a mix of organ and an occasional guitar note from nowhere that denotes that this is not going to be a picture-perfect live album like *Made In Japan*. Nevertheless, this is very fast and proves, if nothing else, that 16 years after the original was recorded, the band had more than enough energy to tackle it. Blackmore's guitar solo is augmented by some new bridgework, which may be ranked among his best recorded live work.

'Strange Kind Of Woman' [incl: 'Jesus Christ Superstar' (Webber, Rice)]
There is a lower-fi quality about this track, which again begs the question, why bother when there are better live versions of this song in DP's recorded canon? Blackmore throws in inviting trills and solos which offer a point of difference to those versions that came before it, and Gillan's voice is in better form on this track, including some good question-and-answer work with Blackmore which leads to a section where they break into 'Jesus Christ Superstar'. It ends with Gillan thanking the audience before a fade-out. Then there is a fade-in with more audience noise and Gillan again thanking the audience. This was already not the greatest of editing jobs.

'Dead Or Alive' (Blackmore, Gillan, Glover)
The fade-in takes us to one of the lesser tracks from *The House Of Blue Light*, although it starts promisingly. A cool jazz blues, probably the most effective since 1972's 'Lazy', is yet another of the band's surprises. It's tantalising and too short, probably culled because of album time constraints, making this another unfortunate production decision. As we get into the song proper, Gillan shows his chops, going higher than on the studio version. Lord and Blackmore trade-off, solo after solo, making this an exciting live version of a full-pace track. If the song itself had more to it, this could really have been something.

'Perfect Strangers' (Blackmore, Gillan, Glover)
In another odd production decision, the track begins with Gillan's opening banter coming from nowhere, giving the sense it was halfway through before the recording started. But once the music starts, it's another thing altogether. Compared to some of the earlier tracks on the album, this one is produced as a power ballad with drums that sound like canons and an organ that swirls. Not even the compression (that makes it sound almost like a mono track) can ruin the magnificence of the music. It's also a joy to hear the audience scream their appreciation when Lord breaks into the signature synth motif across the song. Gillan's vocal almost matches the studio version, although it sounds suspiciously like the vocal is triple-tracked at 1.20. And there is a fabulous note by Gillan at 3.35 that tells of the glory days. It's only a note, but what a note. The song ends with another reference to 'Jesus Christ Superstar' (the second on this album) with a line from his 'Gethsemane', an addition that would stay in every live version of this song from now on.

'Hard Lovin' Woman' (Blackmore, Gillan, Glover) [incl: 'Land Of Hope And Glory' (Elgare)]
In another lazy editing decision, Gillian's many 'thank you's from the last track is faded and then faded up with more of them and, inexplicably, a back-announce. But the song that follows has nothing lazy about it. The band display the same kind of energy as in 'Dead Or Alive' two tracks before. So

fast it is that the details are almost trampled, threatening to turn this lesser album track from *The House Of Blue Light* into an even more average song. But it is this thrash energy that saves it, especially when they slide into 'Under The Gun' before coming back to 'Hard Lovin' Woman' with a vengeance. It's a little too fast for Gillan, who makes the best of it and still manages to get in an amazing variety of tones and screams. Just as well.

'Bad Attitude' (Blackmore, Gillan, Glover, Lord)
Gillan introduces this number with a recital of 'Teddy Bears' Picnic', an early 1900s children's poem. He adds a twist, though, converting the picnic into a drunken gathering apropos of nothing. The big variation from the studio version is when Gillan cuts loose from 2.10. This is followed by a messy interchange (or a bad edit) between organ and guitar before Blackmore grounds everything with a solid solo. Lord jams over the last quarter of the song, and again, things seem to have either been badly recorded or badly edited (or badly played). This performance should never have been allowed anywhere near an LP.

'Knocking At Your Back Door' (Blackmore, Gillan, Glover)
By far the longest track on the album, Lord leads off with some classical piano, including Beethoven's 'Für Elise' (which the audience joins in on) and a jazzy blues interlude, which is again answered by the audience. After the madness of the preceding track, this is a welcome respite, and judging from the audience's cheers, they appreciated it, too. Then, after nearly four minutes we get to the song proper. It doesn't all go well. At about 4.15, the keyboard introduction disappears just as the bass starts, and the bass itself sounds like a wet fish being slapped on a slab. Paice's drums and Blackmore's guitar are excellent, but there's no escaping that it's still a swill of a mix. Gillan has the rare appearance of having lost interest, except for a short scat section right near the end that's too little, too late. The fans would be much better off devoting their time to the original rather than this pale imitation, for it is a second-rate way to finish the first album in this set.

'Child In Time'
The second album comprises more tracks from the band's early years, starting with this Gillan vocal showcase from 1970's *In Rock*. Despite the intervening 18 years, he does the extraordinary highs well, although he shreds a little early on. Lord's solo is so completely divorced from his recorded version that it may feel out of place to *In Rock* fans. Blackmore also takes liberties, but he delivers in spades with a solo that is as athletic as it is original. However, by this stage, the song could be any of the band's fast songs and the 1970 'Child in Time' seems well forgotten until everything stops and we are back in the song again. Gillan takes liberties with the lyrics ('they're killing everyone') and, in the process, kills the wonderful subtlety that made the original what it

was, although from then on, he holds true to his vocal gymnastics of the early days. For that alone, this track is a highlight.

'Lazy'

This blues jam starts with hints of 'Black Night' and 'Smoke On The Water' before jumping into a rather overplayed series of staccato notes before going into 'Lazy'. Unfortunately, by this time, the band seem to be playing for themselves, not the song. Even Lord, the band member who has traditionally been the greatest respecter of the music, inappropriately throws in his oft-used and twee 'Sailor's Hornpipe' byplay. Unlike earlier live versions of this song, this one is relatively short and is not a solo showcase but rather a chance for everyone to do whatever they want. Only Glover and Gillan seem to be on a self-imposed leash, and it's a good thing someone was.

'Space Truckin''

Lord has the job of opening this track and does it with some spacey bits of work. There's not a lot of it, though, and the organ/bass/drum staccato has none of the strength of either the studio or the *Made In Japan* versions. There is a bit of play, with Gillan laughing at one point. If the intention of the album was to show how DP has evolved over the years, this track shows a band willing to experiment, like Paice's short drum solo. This track has been done better on other live albums, but this version shows some daring, at least. It ends with too much of Gillan thanking the audience before the inevitable encore.

'Black Night'

The encore begins with an enticingly soft version of this song's riff, which is instantly picked up by the audience, who starts singing the line before the song even starts. This is one of the better-recorded songs in this mixed bag, with Paice's drums upfront. In a rare case of not listening or not caring, Blackmore's guitar stamps slightly over the beginning of Lord's organ solo. The mix, too, obviously draws down the drums as Gillan talks to the audience, encouraging them to sing the riff. Despite these drawbacks, this is, as always, a masterly encore number.

'Woman From Tokyo' [incl: 'Everyday' (Petty, Hardin)]

It may be the shortest live track on the set, yet the first 45 seconds is taken up with nothing much as Gillan banters about which track this is going to be. The studio version may have been recorded at an unhappy time for the band, but once they start playing, they sound at ease. It morphs into an apparently impromptu version of Buddy Holly's 'Everyday' before Gillan rambles about a TV film on Holly and fades out mid-speech. Decidedly odd. The dross is starting to pile up. Perhaps a single album for this set would have been a smarter move.

'Smoke On The Water'

The inevitable finisher. Gillan tells its story just as he has hundreds of times before. The star, though, is the Blackmore and Lord riff. Blackmore extends his solo right across the riff right up to the chorus. As a variation on the original, it's an interesting document, although it seems like Lord has confused his sound effects, playing the siren and burning effects in the wrong verse. The closing patter spends a lot of time on how great Gillan has found Oslo before the band comes in with some final riffing, giving Gillan a chance to get in some more of his screams. And very good screaming it is, too. And as a good finish as it is, there is a studio-recorded highlight to come.

'Hush' (Joe South)

It obviously seemed a good idea at the time. Since the album was mostly live recordings of existing material, why not do something DP had never done before: re-record a song performed by an earlier version of the band? Twenty years had passed since DP had their first international hit with this Joe South song, so someone decided this was just the thing to go for. In his autobiography, Gillan says he was against the idea:

> Adding 'Hush' was (for me) the strangest idea of all. Nobody has yet owned up to that idea, although I did try to get it across that Rod Evans could have done a much better job than I managed with the newer version. An original is always best!

The remake starts similarly to the original with an animal howl. When the band kicks in, it immediately feels looser and funkier. Despite his misgivings, Gillan shows nothing but enthusiasm, including his scream at the end of the verses and a few sexy 'urgh's. Blackmore's guitar is revitalised, and the drum sound is superb. The high quality of this studio recording has an unfortunate side effect, though: it plays up the contrast with the poor sound of the rest of the set.

The single's video clip is the band's most American-influenced, as a man and a woman drive their convertibles. And that's really about all that happens. The video moves at a fair skip, matching the music, but it is nonsense to the lyrics.

So, this is a contemporary take on an old hit, although the keyboardist, drummer and guitarist were the same for both. It is an achievement that it turned out this well when the band was amid an implosion.

Despite what Ian Gillan might say, there is nothing to be ashamed of here. It is sharp, horny and fun, making the top 100 in both the UK and the US but going nowhere near matching the success of the 1968 version. Interestingly, Gillan would not veto the song popping up in the band's live sets over the ensuing years. It was still being performed in 2024.

Slaves & Masters (1990)

Personnel
Joe Lynn Turner: vocals
Richie Blackmore: guitars
Jon Lord: keyboards
Roger Glover: bass, keyboards
Ian Paice: drums and percussion
Record label: RCA
Recorded at Greg Rike Productions, Florida, US; Sountec Studios, Connecticut, US; Power Station, New York, US, between February and June 1990
Produced by Roger Glover
Release date: 5 October 1990
Highest chart places: UK: 45, US: 87
Running time: 46:51

Album Facts

This album proves how one member can change the whole tone of a group. In this case, new singer Joe Lynn Turner. Gillan had been fired after a band meeting in which the singer lost his temper and called Bruce Payne, the group's manager, 'fucking useless'. Blackmore told *Metal Magazine*'s Anders Tengner in 1993 that this was the last straw:

> I said to the rest of the band: 'What's Ian doing other than drinking and getting crazy?' So I turned around and said, 'I'd really rather not carry on with this arrangement. Let's get somebody else in to sing something properly.' So they went along with it.

Lord may have gone along with it, but only a few years later, he told *Keyboard* magazine's Robert Doerschuk that Gillan's dismissal was wrongheaded:

> Somebody stepped on the self-destruct button, and we decided to change singers. That was, if I can coin a phrase, a fucking stupid and idiotic thing to do. I don't know why we did it, but we did.

Idiotic, perhaps, but the Gillan milk was truly spilt, and it left DP with a big but simple decision. Carry on or pack it in. Colin Hart wrote in his autobiography that each member had said over the previous six years that if one member left, then they would not continue, but now that that situation arose, the musketeer-ish attitude was ditched, and they decided to find a replacement singer. Australians John Farnham and Jimmy Barnes were considered, as was Rainbow and Black Sabbath frontman Ronnie James Dio. In the end, Blackmore suggested Joe Lynn Turner, who was Blackmore's last singer in Rainbow. Turner told the author that he had been considering jobs with Foreigner and Bad Company when serendipity intervened:

> I swear, like it was a stroke of lightning that Colin Hart called... and said we want you to come up to Vermont and dive into a Purple rehearsal. We're looking for a singer. So, I was weighing the odds between Bad Company and Purple. And, of course, Purple was one of my favourite bands.

Hart says in his autobiography it all clicked when Turner got to Vermont:

> He stepped right up to the plate and strutted his stuff. Smiles all round, one singer delivered.

Putting Turner in the band was a big turnaround for Blackmore, who had told Geoff Barton in 1984 that he thought Turner was too smooth to sing rock. The appointment was also divisive among fans. Some, resentful of Gillan's treatment and fearful that Blackmore was employing a power play, disdainfully called this version of DP 'Deep Rainbow'. This was a trifle unfair. Blackmore had suggested, but not insisted, on Turner's appointment, but once ensconced in DP, Turner did not help his own case by making some characteristic shoot-from-the-hip statements about Gillan, including saying he didn't want to sing 'someone else's drivel'. Gillan's autobiography cites Turner saying of him: 'Ian Gillan? Let's not speak ill of the dead.' Turner told the author that this was actually a Blackmore line and that with his 'drivel' comment, he was only trying to be funny.

But the fact was Blackmore was now free of his nemesis and there was, for a time, fresh air. After relatively smooth recording sessions for *Slaves & Masters*, the band turned to touring, which started in the Czech Republic and then went to Hungary, Croatia, France, Germany, Scandinavia and the UK before the US leg. Apart from some audience calls for Gillan in quiet moments, Colin Hart told the author the European leg was well received by the audiences, but in the US, there were some unsettling signs. Only eight shows were booked, and in Japan, their agent, Mr Udo, could only secure four concert dates. Although they were much better received in Brazil, Hart says any optimism had evaporated by September 1991:

> The *Slaves & Masters* trek stuttered to a halt with one-off shows in Poland, Athens and Israel. The feeling in the band was awful. No energy, no bright eyes, any future?

So what went wrong? Perhaps it was that Gillan and Turner were as different as two rock singers could possibly be. Where Gillan was sharp in style and words, Turner oozed smoothness. And his pop nous may have been a little too pop nous for traditional DP fans worried that their heroes were getting into what might be Foreigner territory.

The album did not do particularly well either, charting well lower than any of the Gillan albums. The choice of the American Turner was not accepted well by

UK audiences (*Slaves & Masters* only reached number 45 there). We should note that the album did get into the top 100 stateside, which was the last DP set to do so, but the overall sales drop and the paucity of tour bookings meant it was no surprise that this lineup would produce only one album.

Paice, however, refuses to speak ill of Turner. In April 2017, he told *Uncut* magazine's John Robinson that 'he may not have been the right guy, but he stopped the ship from sinking.'

An interesting comment, considering Gillan, in his autobiography, says he suspects it was Paice, not Blackmore, who was behind the push to get him out of the band in the first place. As with all things DP, life was complicated.

Album Cover

In keeping with previous albums, there is no band member on the cover; instead, there is a reference to 'Fortuneteller', with the centre dominated by a crystal ball which contains a plethora of items, including the DP reunion logo. There's also a *The Twilight Zone*-style eerie eye, a truck that could be turning into a face, melting instruments and records, and a few other bits and pieces. The crystal ball is being read by two sets of hands with bright red fingernails. In all, it is baffling, a little like the cover for *Nobody's Perfect*. The general idea for the design came from Glover, and only he must know what he was thinking.

The back cover continues the crystal ball theme with ethereal fingers coming from the clouds over the ball, which is much less interesting on this side, containing just the track listing. Across the top, as if watching the clairvoyant session from a balcony, is the band. In keeping with the style of the video from 'King Of Dreams', the monochrome band looks at its best: slim, dark-haired and interested. They are also mostly bare-armed, and these arms, in contrast to the darkness of the background, could be used to make a set of hieroglyphic symbols.

All tracks by Blackmore, Turner and Glover (unless otherwise noted)

'King Of Dreams'

This track, which was the Turner DP's first single, epitomised the new band as smooth and sultry. This is emphasised in its music video. Set in a fairground, a singletted young man flirts with a girl who looks suspiciously underage. But it's the tracking shots of the band in this video that speak the loudest. Taking a sabbatical from being street rockers, all band members are dressed in Turner and Blackmore's signature pop-rock black uniform. Even Glover, the self-acknowledged hippy, forwent his grungy duds. Turner told the author he was the one who pushed for the change:

> At my expense, I said you guys gotta look like a band. You guys are legends, and you dress like bums.

The new stage wear is augmented by plenty of power stances and close-ups of Turner's face. DP seemed intent on reaching for a younger demographic, which is probably why Jon Lord, then 49 years old, only gets in frame twice. It's significant that after Turner left the band, Glover went back to his former attire.

The song itself is a good 'un, though, starting with Lord's now-trademark brooding opening synths. Drums, bass and guitar join in, and up to this point, this is classic DP. It is when Turner comes in that we know this is something else. Instead of the Gillan wails, we have more vocal restraint, less aggression, and a tone that would never have fitted on *In Rock* or *Machine Head* but one that is enticing, nonetheless. Turner does use his upper register, but not until late in the song.

Blackmore told *Guitar World*'s Mordechai Kleidermacher he deliberately wanted the song to have space:

> That's why it's very sparse. I didn't want to just show off some trick I'd learned at the music store on Saturday morning.

In all, it was a promising dawn to what would prove to be a very short new era.

'The Cut Runs Deep' (Blackmore, Turner, Glover, Lord, Paice)

This was the second track the band played with Turner in the semi-audition in Vermont. Turner says Blackmore played a riff, then Lord joined in, and he added lyrics to what was essentially a jam. It was this synergy that led the band to ask him to join.

It starts well with a classical-style piano that is joined by a line from Blackmore's guitar. Turner uses his range in this piece, though by now, it's becoming apparent there's no comparison to Gillan's extraordinary octaves. Turner's chorus features himself multi-tracked and answers his phrases with his own lower-scale retorts. His lyrics don't really go much deeper beyond being a criticism of a betraying lover:

> Turning the knife
> How much can I bleed
> The cut runs deep

There is a traditional DP vibe following the guitar solo, where drums, bass and guitar improvise a section before the final organ solo. By this point, the song has turned into a soloing showcase. But this doesn't cover the fact that it's a jam; a very good, polished jam, but a jam, nonetheless.

'Fire In The Basement' (Blackmore, Turner, Glover, Lord, Paice)

A music magazine once told Ian Paice that he was a jazz drummer in a rock band. Paice seemed to be chuffed by this. Turner told the author he certainly loved Paice's feel:

> The swing, you know. He had a way of swinging everything. It doesn't matter if it's hard rock or anything. It's almost jazz. But it's not.

If this business about a jazz drummer in a rock band is true, then this song is the perfect example. Paice manages to infuse a jazz/shuffle feel in a way that's as athletic as anything he's done since the reformation, bearing similarities to 1969's 'Wring That Neck', just heavier and with words. Turner goes as far as to call this the 'Lazy' of this album.

The lyrics are in the Gillan rude style, and Turner admits it is indeed all about sex and little else, although surprisingly, perhaps, he credits the story to Glover, not himself. He sings of breaking into a house and having a range of sexual experiences, which seems rather predatory, given she loses her innocence in the process. He doesn't even know her name. Thus, the theme is somewhat unsavoury (not unlike Gillan's 'Sacre Bleu' from *Future Shock,* except at least in that case, the offender gets his comeuppance), and it's a shame because the song is a nice turn for the band who let rip, Lord especially. He throws in glissandos aplenty in his solos, relishing the fast tempo. There is a lovely pianissimo section three-quarters in, which allows some tasteful Blackmore fingerpicking.

This all makes for one of the strongest songs on the album. If the lyrics were a little less toilet wall, it could have been a DP classic.

'Truth Hurts'

The first of three contiguous slow tracks on the album, this plays to Turner's strengths. After the lively naughtiness of the preceding track, 'Truth Hurts' goes into a very different zone. This one oozes the pathos of a person who has been dumped by their lover. Turner told the author that the reviewers didn't understand the truth of the song. He was going through a divorce at the time, and he was reflecting on the 'misgivings and wrongs that we create for each other.'

Turner takes us through the whole proceeding in six verses, from the protagonist's initial shock to anger, to depression and resignation, to self-pride, and finally, hope. That's a lot in one ballad. Interestingly, the stanzas contain some repeated chorus refrains, which are a blend of chorus and verse.

Turner may not have the range of Gillan, but his use of light and shade here is refreshing. He gives himself so much headroom that when he needs to take it up a few notes or give us a good scream, he can.

The music is enchanting with its use of string synth throughout. Blackmore joins in about halfway through to give a solo that is one of his best on this set.

So then, interesting lyrical technique, great singing, lovely guitar and powerful synths. Yet, it doesn't all add up to a great track. Producer Glover put all the pieces in place, but I wonder how many listeners will repeat this one or go straight on to the next track. I'm guessing the latter. As much as

Glover and Turner would wish it to be otherwise, there's a lack of emotional involvement here, and that is a real shame.

'Breakfast In Bed'

This is in a similar category to 'Truth Hurts' in that all the elements are there again, but it's not enough to equate to greatness. Part of the issue could be that we get anonymous drumming and bass, although Glover does throw in a few embellishments. Even Blackmore's lines feel like he's done it all before. The opening has a slow synth almost identical to that of the preceding track. Why didn't someone pick that up?

The words are clever, though:

Woke up this morning, the rain coming down
Washing the sin from the streets
Sometimes I feel like I'm losing ground
Just trying to make ends meet

So, it is a song about another loser, written by Turner on a rainy morning. In a way, it could be a sequel to the emotional break-up tragedy from the previous track. Our man is still down, but now he's looking for someone new, promising not to be too much trouble (hardly a great selling point), and by the last verse, he has even resorted to pleading. The album is certainly moving downbeat.

The meaning of the title words could be anything. Perhaps, literally, he wants someone to take care of him. Gillan would have it as a euphemism for you-know-what. The truth probably is that the words seemed to work as a chorus phrase, so they kept them. There's a power ballad to come. Let's hope everyone cheers up a bit.

'Love Conquers All'

Just when the album needs something upbeat, we get a ballad that has a tone of moving on, yet the words, for the third time in a row, tell of someone still shattered by bad love. At least this time, they're trying to get themselves out of the mess. The all-conquering love of the title sits strangely among the rest of the lyrics. It seems that Turner is telling us that love hasn't conquered; it's been hung, drawn and quartered and he's hoping it will now overcome all this turmoil. Of course, this may be reading too deeply into what is just a song of hope.

Turner told the author that Lord was not a fan of the song. He thought it too syrupy. And it's true that the backing is, for the most part, anonymous. The guitar solo sounds like it could have been played by any lead guitarist in any middle-to-top band of the time. It begins, again, with Lord's synth, but this time, it's quite a beautiful opening. It would have been interesting to see what would have resulted if these strings had stayed the course instead of disappearing come the first verse. What we are left with is a song that is well-written, nicely arranged, impeccably played, and strongly produced but, once again, never really touches.

Released as a single, the track came in a limited-edition vinyl disc that was in the shape of the DP logo. Its sleeve, designed by Shoot That Tiger, showed a blond woman with a DP logo tattooed on her arm, wrapped only in a purple drape. It was the 1980s, indeed.

'Fortuneteller' (Blackmore, Turner, Glover, Lord, Paice)

For the fourth time in a row, we have synths starting the song (it's getting a bit boring now, Jon), leading into a picking guitar before another story of a man who is alone. Paice must've been pulling out his hair by this point, for once again, he is given nothing much to do, nor is he given the space to drive the music. Roger Glover was famously told when he first joined the band in 1969 to just keep out of the way of Paice's drumming. In 1990, nobody had to keep out of the drummer's way.

This is not to say the music has no verve. The chorus has Lord powering in the style of an orchestra of cellos that would be explored further on the next album, and this fits the song's brooding ambience. Turner told the author that what he loved about Lord was that 'he knew where to be where Blackmore was not'. This is most evident on this track, where Lord and Blackmore display a synergy while respecting each other's space. About 90 seconds from the end, there is a glorious build-up of the music that leads into a Turner wail that sounds eerily like David Coverdale.

This time around, our man has gone to a clairvoyant to find out if there is any love on the horizon. He's still not having a great deal of luck in love, and he asks the fortune teller for help. It's just that he does it again and again, making story development sadly non-existent.

Once again, it's a nice tune, but it could have been so much more. Gillan's lyrical contrast and sense of humour are starting to be missed. At least the pace varies on the next one.

'Too Much Is Not Enough' (Turner, Held, Greenwood)

And this Turner song is a change of pace indeed, and it's a change with real oomph. The chorus is a thunderous blend of guitar and voice but mostly belongs to Lord's triumphant blasts, while Paice is allowed for the first time in a while to do what he does best: drive and propel. Blackmore's solo is lively and far more inspired than in the preceding tracks. This song straddles power rock with pop sensibilities in a way not dissimilar to Robert Palmer's 1986 hit 'Addicted To Love'. As such, it's a slightly dated attempt at the genre, but the musicianship pulls it through. It's also one of the few tunes on the album that could bear listening on rotation. And it's also Turner's best vocal performance here.

DP purists raised on *Machine Head* and *In Rock* will probably always hate it, and it certainly has dated as the product of the 1980s that it is. But it's no

'Maxwell's Silver Hammer'. Listen closely enough and all the DP players are doing what they've always done and done too rarely on this album.

'Wicked Ways' (Blackmore, Turner, Glover, Lord, Paice)
This is close to the classic DP, especially when we get to the middle, where there's a half-time change of pace, which is one of the most breathtaking moments on the album. Blackmore and Lord trade-off daringly as of days of old, with Paice and Glover blasting behind. Space is given and gladly taken.

Although Turner's vocal contributions would not be on the next album, this part of this track is a pointer to the sound they would be aiming for the next time they go into the studio. Turner delivers a fabulous gymnastic vocal throughout. It must be said that the lyrics are the same 'I want you, satisfy me, let's go to heaven' type of thing, but in the way they are sung, they sound profound.

'Slow Down Sister' (Blackmore, Turner, Glover, Lord, Paice) (2012 bonus track)
This extra track is like nothing else from the *Slaves & Masters* sessions. Early on, there's a sense of 'Stormbringer'. Then we get into the stadium rock of the early 1980s. Even the wail of the words sounds like a hook from a Kiss anthem from the period, with a guitar not unlike Paul Stanley. This was obviously an exploration of styles. However, somebody must have said that there was enough kowtowing to current trends, so the track didn't make the album cut. Quite right, too, although it's interesting to hear what would have happened if DP had developed this tangent. As it is, it sounds mostly like everyone else. It's the nature of this kind of anthem.

The Battle Rages On (1993)

Personnel
Ian Gillan: vocals, congas
Richie Blackmore: guitars
Jon Lord: keyboards, backing vocals
Roger Glover: bass, backing vocals
Ian Paice: drums
Record label: RCA
Recorded at Greg Rike Studios, Florida, US; Bearsville Studios, NY, US; Red Rooster Studios, Germany, between May 1992 and March 1993
Produced by Thom Panunzio/Roger Glover
Release date: 2 July 1993
Highest chart places: UK: 21, US: 192
Running time: 50:17

Album Facts

The story of this album was as convoluted as it was inevitable. *Slaves & Masters*' relative failure led the record company to push Blackmore to allow Gillan back into the fold (rumours were of a $1 million offer to Blackmore, although this has never been confirmed publicly). Turner told the author that an offer was made that couldn't be refused:

> BMG came along to management and offered an enormous amount of money to get Gillan back in the band and I guess money talks and nobody walks. I was used to doing one-offs. So I just went in with both guns blazing and said look, we're going to write great songs and come up with a great album and let the chips fall.

In the end, they didn't follow Turner's way. There was more to it than just the lack of sales success. In June 2018, Glover, who was producing the new album, told *Classic Rock*'s Paul Rees there was dissension about the Turner direction from all quarters, not just the record company:

> During the course of the recording, it became obvious that we should part. I don't want to go into the reasons why, but we ended up with a lot of backing tracks and no singer.

By the time this decision was made, there had been a lot of session and writing time with Turner, who, at this point, still believed he was the singer of DP. But he told the author that claims he had laid down his lyrics were not true:

> What we had were tracks, and I had what we call scats over most of the stuff… scats... skeletons... yabba yabba dabba do. That sort of stuff.

'One Man's Meat' [see that track's notes below] is one song that gives an idea of what the album would have sounded like if Turner's scats had been allowed to develop. Turner later repurposed it for one of his albums, and the sound is very different. It's an interesting listen but academic. Turner was dismissed and Glover was given the task of bringing his old friend Gillan back. Gillan told *Metal Magazine*'s Anders Tengner in 1993 that after his firing, he had promised himself that he would sooner slit his throat than play in 'that band' again. Three years had softened his view, for he quickly accepted Glover's offer. In his autobiography, Gillan said it wasn't until he started working again with Glover that he realised he was not being invited back into DP; rather, he was being auditioned. He obviously bit the bullet, finishing the lyrics for what would become *The Battle Rages On*. Those lyrics are tough. They have plenty of talk of battles and killing and give a feeling of angst to much of the album. It doesn't help that Gillan sings his lungs out from start to finish, adding to the bombastic feel. Blackmore told Jerry Bloom that he didn't like what Gillan did to the vocals:

> If you heard just the backing tracks, they sounded really good. Then, when the vocals got put on [thumbs down].

Despite Blackmore's feelings, this is a set loaded with great moments, with some of the most interesting music of the reunion so far, and Gillan was to go as far as to say in an interview on the *Come Hell Or High Water* DVD that he considered this to be one of the best produced DP albums, and his favourite since *Machine Head*. Lord agreed at the time, saying that the album sparkled and was a return to form:

> We wanted to show that we could deliver better things than *Slaves & Masters*, which was really not a Deep Purple album at all. It carried the name, but the sleeve was deceiving.

The highlights mean that this cannot be anywhere near one of their worst albums. It's just that it's nowhere near one of their best. Turner and Blackmore later referred to it as 'The Cattle Grazes On'.

Obviously, hell hath no fury…

Album Cover

This James Grashow artwork places the reunion logo centre place on a cover that owes more to a Whitesnake design than what we have been used to from DP. But a closer look tells a story. A two-headed dragon, entwined around the logo, is about to attack its other head, which is at the end of its own tail. Whoever came up with the idea for this was either remarkably prescient, having a huge lend, or both. Whatever its genesis, this front cover fitted the album very well, not just for the internal band struggles but also for the nature of Gillan's somewhat fighting words sprinkled throughout. The rear cover is plain backside stuff, with a track listing and production credits and a cryptic figure on the left of a ten-armed bat hanging onto a skewed compass, which itself has a crescent below it, over a series of faded dragon images. It is about as baffling as the front cover is obvious. By the way, that DP logo, like Blackmore, would never feature again on a DP studio album, although it continues to be used on band merchandise.

All tracks by Blackmore, Gillan and Glover (unless otherwise noted)

'The Battle Rages On' (Blackmore, Gillan, Lord, Paice)
In keeping with the album name and Gillan's conflicted feelings about the reunion, we have an opening track that cleverly puts it all into song. Like on so many tracks on the previous album, this starts with string synths, but here, in the context of the band's situation, its ominous tone tells us that a change is coming. Then it hits. A barrage of sudden, tight staccato drums, bass and guitar lead into Gillan singing what could well be his own story:

> Been so many words so much to say
> Words are not enough to keep the guns at bay
> Some live in fear some do not
> Some gamble everything on who gets the final shot

Strong words delivered in a way uncharacteristic of the man. He sounds as if he is pleading and, unlike on his last DP album, he's given his voice some headroom for moments like when he belts out the song's title. This is a lyric that is Gillan at his most pensive, although, at first listening, it could sound like he's advocating violence. Of course, the lyrics call for no such thing. Rather, they reflect on how humankind has gotten it wrong for too long.

The music, as it's written, doesn't vary much. In lesser hands, it could be nothing more than a fast drudge. In fact, Paice told Craig Gruber from *Everyone Loves Guitar* that it took a long time to get the slightly shuffling groove right:

> We were getting nowhere. It just wasn't working. We kept soldiering on. And a little light went on and the drum part changed completely and all of a sudden, it was working. For those five minutes, we just hit it. We couldn't do it again. And that became the master.

The song succeeds because, in that take, everyone grabs it by the neck and treats it in a manner akin to 1973's song 'Burn'. They are just as tight, enthusiastic and inventive. Only Lord takes a while to get into it, happy to do no more than fill in with keyboards for the first part of the song. Blackmore produces an attacking solo that is so uncharacteristically short that it seems like he has accidentally pulled out his plug. Lord does get his moment after this, though, trading lines with Blackmore as the rhythm section punch and pivot across them. They finally all work together to give a crescendo before the whole thing ends with a percussive whack. It's all-new, dynamic and musically masterful stuff. Welcome back, DP.

'Lick It Up'

Only a few years after the band Kiss had turned the words of this title into an anthem to oral sex, DP does the same thing, but a little more obliquely:

> I don't want your money
> I don't want your soul
> I don't need a reason
> I just want to get right down and lick it up

Obtuse, indeed, until they eventually lead to no other interpretation but of the sexual kind. It's a throwback to the dense but vacuous lyrics of his Gillan days. And just when we thought he'd grown out of all this.

This is one of the few cases where it was obvious that Gillan's lyric had been retrofitted to a song written for Turner. Even so, Gillan does throw his all into this rather minor song.

The music, a mid-tempo grunge, is pretty thin. With its simple riff, it would like to be in the genre of one of the less busy tracks from *In Rock* but never gets close. Lord contributes a clavinet but nothing else. Paice, however, is given space to show some of his bass drum virtuosity. And let's not forget his fine roll at the start. Good bits that just don't add up to a worthwhile whole.

'Anya' (Blackmore, Gillan, Glover, Lord)

One of the centrepieces of the album. The lovely classically influenced guitar opening is an inkling of the music Blackmore will pursue when he leaves the band soon after. He is joined by Lord's strings in a touching few moments before it all erupts into something far, far heavier but strangely, with a sense of the medieval. Lord uses a wave station sample of a cimbalom, marked on the instrument as a clavichord. He told Robert Doerschuk it gave the effect of a string being hit with a hammer, so it sounded slightly out-of-tune.

It is a pumping piece loaded with interesting twists and turns, each driven by either guitar or synth or both, and everything melds well, although it's interesting to hear at one point Blackmore stealing his own riff from Rainbow's 'Stranded' from the *Bent Out Of Shape* album. Glover's bass and Paice's drums never deviate, laying down the most solid of backbones for others to dance on. And dance they most certainly do with abandon, never once interfering with each other. Only a band with the skill of DP could pull this off.

Gillan's lyric gives the song an extra, mysterious layer. Is he talking about a Scandinavian freedom fighter? A gypsy? A refugee? It's only in the last paragraph that he reveals the clue that she is a girl he loves (who could still be any of the above).

Then there's the ending that takes us back to the classical opening, this time with a harpsichord/harp to close it out.

It is no surprise that the band will play the masterly 'Anya' live over the next few years.

'Talk About Love'

The album now gets straight back into the hard and heavy. This has some interesting changes and quite a bit of verve, but it also has that almost inexpressible quality of being a little alienating. Perhaps it's the vocal that charges over Blackmore's work, like a lyric thrown onto a set backing. There's no light, just heaps of dark shade.

Not that the lyric demands this attention. It's a story lyric that has all the Gillan art in it, cleverly flitting from aside to aside, but in the end, he just wants to talk with his woman, and the subject is love. However, Gillan sings this as if it's as important as Shakespeare.

This is close to the shortest track on the album and probably just as well.

'Time To Kill'

In his autobiography, Gillan wrote that this song was disliked by Blackmore, yet the riff-based track starts with sharp guitar work, and when Gillan enters, it is with a warning:

> Consider your position, position your defence.

This might be something interesting, then. But not so. It immediately starts to trip over itself with a mixing of metaphors that frankly reeks of overkill.

> Feeding speculators on a downhill gravy train
> Like vultures ripping out the eyes to reach the dying brain

From here, things settle into a much more coherent pondering on the meaning of life and the need for acceptance of things as they are. This is where Gillan's tendency to throw his all into his singing can be misconstrued. No, the lyric is not about violence, death or anything of the sort. The poor man is just saying he needs a rest.

The words meld well with the backing track, which is about as simple as anything Blackmore has ever composed. Like the song before it, there are some lovely sections, like Blackmore's short solo and the lead into Lord's solo towards the end (at last, the pianist is getting some airtime), but it's not enough to make it anything like a classic DP track.

'Ramshackle Man'

This is one of the last exuberant all-band recordings of this incarnation of DP. In an album where resentment was running high, here, there is nothing but a feeling of joy. This track cuts no new ground musically and its inspiration could well have come from Booker T and the MGs' 'Green Onions' with its simple repetitive organ refrain, but the band still makes it their own. Blackmore picks over the top of the song like a man inspired as Lord exchanges leads with him. He even throws in a fabulous tiger roar-like glissando at the end of his first organ solo.

Gillan is equally clever, telling the story of a self-confessed loser, using his best contrasting imagery:

My clothes don't fit and I have no point of view
I've got a bad reputation but I don't believe it's true.

His voice is in fine form, and just when you think he is pushing his limits, he goes impressively harder in the last verse. And there's a perfectly placed scream thrown in as a segue between solos. The back end is given to Blackmore as the rest of the band whips up a frenzy. This album might not always cook, but it does right here with passion and an obvious love of what they were playing, which could make one wonder that if they did more of this kind of music, things might not have gone south.

'A Twist In The Tale'

A fast rocker that could define the term 'punishing', this track revisits the band's talent as speed kings. Starting apace and staying there, the track still allows for some contrast. It lets up just after each chorus, but only for a few seconds before charging back into it again. There's a middle-eight of sorts, followed by a solid guitar solo. Once that's out of the way, it's back to full tilt. Lord's synths bring in the song's only slow bit, which has some lovely guitar interplay. Then it ends just as it was getting interesting.

The most fascinating aspect of the song is the lyrics. The man who earlier sang about oral sex now returns to his criticism writing. The subject this time is someone sitting high on a hill while the world revolves around them. Given the state of the relationship between the singer and the guitarist at that time, the subtext is clear. To everyone but the guitarist, that is. Like 'Smooth Dancer' from *Who Do We Think We Are*, he must have been totally unaware of what Gillan was singing about as he played underneath.

It's all strangely unengaging, but the band must have enjoyed playing it. This song was to feature in the live setlist for some time to come.

'Nasty Piece Of Work' (Blackmore, Gillan, Glover, Lord)

This is the most progressive track for quite some time, led by Lord right from his powerful first notes. When Blackmore enters the fray, it is what it should be: a fitting addition, not just an adornment. The same goes for Lord's solo, which fits in with everyone: guitar, drums, bass, voice, as in the early 1970s. He tosses out glissandos that are barely audible but so definitely propulsive. Thrilling even.

Unlike some earlier work on the album, Gillan's voice (or voices) fits the mid-tempo backing to perfection, his words ranging from half to double-time. Like Lord, he plays at it, including a good old-fashioned high note at 3.30 that comes from nowhere, goes nowhere, lasts only two seconds, and would thrill the heart of any DP fan of old. The lyrics fit the menacing music, with phrases like: 'I can give you pain'; 'gonna bring you down'; 'bad luck is my game'; 'dragging in the dirt'; 'driving into the ground'; 'crawling across the floor'; 'demons' (of both disorder and misfortune). You get the picture. It's dark yet demands repeated listening.

The song also fits perfectly with the track to follow, making a short two-track interlude that is one of the highlights, not just for the album but for the band.

'Solitaire'

This is a mid-tempo song like no other in the DP catalogue; in fact, it's a song that would probably not be found on any hard rock album. This a Blackmore song that has more in common with something to be expected from the Joe Lynn Turner DP or Rainbow, exemplified by its majestic keyboard interludes. A double, possibly triple, tracked Gillan keeps it low key in the verses, opening up as he leads up to the choruses even if he never sounds quite like he believes in his own lyrics, which are clever, by the way. In all, it is one of the band's more successful experimental entries. If a single song can make an album essential, this is it. DP purists might think differently, though.

'One Man's Meat'

This is the track that allows a direct comparison between the Turner and Gillan versions of the band. Turner would keep Blackmore's riff and the bulk of the song as the basis of 'Stroke Of Midnight' from his *Second Hand Life* album. It works better for Turner, with a melody and voice that is less strident and less terse, although the booming drums have dated his version terribly.

DP decided to put 'One Man's Meat' at the end of this album, after the three high-end tracks. This mid-tempo piece allows a respectful space for both singer and guitarist, with Lord the only one who is left in the shadow for the most part; his keyboards obviously wallpaper bar some small work in the spaces. He does get to shine at the end of the song but is quickly faded out just as he seems to be warming up. Given the album's not overlong run time (50 minutes), producers Panunzio and Glover could have allowed the album to finish with a Lord masterclass. It was not to be, and the album is the lesser for it.

The words are either downright sexual or a musical permission to be yourself, a heavy version of John Lennon's 'Whatever Gets You Through The Night'. It could also just be a scream for freedom from a man not enjoying this band business; after all, Glover was to say that when Blackmore left soon after, it was the end of a ten-year headache. The times could not have been as good as they sounded at times on this hot and cold album.

This would be the last track to be released from the Gillan/Blackmore version of DP, so perhaps it's fitting that it owes so much to their heavy beginning together. It's not their greatest heavy collaboration that would go to 'Speed King' or 'Highway Star', but it's no disgrace either.

A new era now beckons.

Come Hell Or High Water (1994)

Personnel
Ian Gillan: vocals
Richie Blackmore: guitars
Jon Lord: keyboards
Roger Glover: bass
Ian Paice: drums and percussion
Record label: BMG
Recorded at Hanns-Martin-Schleyer-Halle, Stuttgart, Germany, on 16 October 1993; Birmingham NEC, Birmingham, UK, on 9 November 1993
Produced by Pat Regan
Release date: 2 November 1994
Highest chart places: Japan: 30, UK: did not chart, US: did not chart
Running time: 77:19

Album Facts

It started as a great idea: with the guitarist and the singer finally making up, record a live version of the band as it is now. And why not go further by putting the recording on both DVD and CD, so the public could be given a document of a band now running on five wheels? The problem was that they had not made up, and so bad were things in the band room that only a week after the recording, Blackmore walked out permanently. So instead of a joyful, all is forgiven document, we have the opposite, a group in disintegration. In his autobiography, Gillan says after an unfortunate opening track [see 'Highway Star' below], Blackmore started on a campaign of 'knocking the songs about, ending early, taking lumps out, and generally leaving me stranded whenever possible.' It is no wonder that Paice shouted to the audience at the end of one of the concerts, 'We owe you a hell of a lot'.

There is also little wonder the album became a rare critical failure, ranking one out of five in the *AllMusic* ratings. This is unfortunate because it's an entertaining concert, and the DVD shows the whole band engaged for a lot of the time. Despite the dramas and his emotional turmoil, Gillan puts in one of his most interesting and animated performances.

This is where the album is most important. It shows Gillan's personal growth. Only a few years before, he had thrown the infamous tantrum that got him fired. Here, he shows a remarkable restraint for the good of the band. From here on, Gillan would display an attitude of one for all.

Album Cover

The cover is simple but elegant and, importantly, makes it clear that this is a live album. The band are shown mid-song with a sleeveless Gillan in centre frame, his mouth pouting a la David Coverdale, and long hair flying, dramatically backlit by a yellow stage light. He is flanked by Blackmore on the right and Glover on the left. On the CD, Lord and Paice are unseen, but on some DVD versions, the shot is wider, and they are seen on the very extremities. The font for the band name is the same as the one on *The Battle Rages On*, and the album title is done in an amended Times New Roman style, which gives it a gothic hint. On the back cover, Gillan dominates again, in mid-pose as half a grinning Paice looks on. Again, Lord doesn't make the cut. Underneath is the track listing and production credits. It's interesting that the quality of the different versions of the cover differ: some have the light colours skewed from orange to red, and Gillan's backlight is green instead of yellow.

All tracks by Blackmore, Gillan, Glover, Lord and Paice (unless otherwise noted)

'Highway Star'

Paice starts this traditional opener under Glover's 16th note line, with Lord filling in on the organ for a beginning that becomes very extended. But something is missing. As Gillan explains in his autobiography, Blackmore has refused to come onstage. It is remarkable that Lord so successfully fills the hole left by the guitar. Eventually, Blackmore shows up, just in time for his solo, as a relieved Gillan points to him. Blackmore's solo is extraordinary, but he stops when he sees a camera operator across the stage. Then we have the spectacle of the guitarist going to the amp between the drummer and the organ, picking up a glass of water and throwing the contents across the back of stage right. He then points in the direction where the water has gone before resuming his solo. Later, Blackmore tried to explain his antics to Jerry Bloom, saying he had been promised the cameras would not be onstage:

> I have a thing about it. It's not fair to these kids who have paid their money to sit and watch the back of some guy's head with a camera. I got all uppity about it.

Colin Hart disputes Blackmore's claim about the cameras being intruders, telling the author that Blackmore had agreed to the plan for two on-stage handheld cameras in a meeting with Hart in the guitarist's kitchen one morning before the start of the tour.

The water tantrum would have slipped benignly into DP chaos folklore except for the fact that when Gillan went backstage to investigate, he found the water had drenched his wife Bron, who had burst into tears. In his autobiography, Gillan says his reaction was: 'I am now going to kill him, probably with a very slow bullet called my right arm' but was talked out of it by his wife and resumed singing as if nothing had happened.

The audience screams just as loudly as usual at the end, but there's no doubt this song's performance was the nadir of the band's live career. Glover later said he was embarrassed and furious. Lord, in an interview conducted for the album's DVD counterpart, said he was also angry and that he had to work hard to keep the energy up because of what had happened. But they soldiered on through their long set.

'Black Night'

Blackmore, who had left the stage at the end of the previous song, shows up late again, letting Lord play the classic riff alone for quite a while before coming in to take over. Once he plays his solos, he leaves again before the end of the song. Ironically, Blackmore's slackness seems to drive the other band members, who all deliver strong performances.

'Twist In The Tale' (Blackmore, Gillan, Glover)

Things get back on track for this *The Battle Rages On* track. Blackmore adds some interesting turns to the original and melds with Lord as they trade lead breaks and work together for the song's main motif. All seems forgiven.

'Perfect Strangers' (Blackmore, Gillan, Glover)

This version of this reunion song is very good, bringing the power of the album track to the stage and then some. Gillan adds to his studio version, singing it out as if he has suddenly found an extra meaning in his own words. Lord also plays it up with some great keyboard work. Of course, it all finishes with his now-customary *Jesus Christ Superstar* line, and then, perhaps surprisingly, Blackmore throws in a fabulous final bit of guitar business reminiscent of the band's glory days.

'Anyone's Daughter'

Good-natured banter by Gillan (very good-natured considering the circumstances) includes an introduction to the band's percussionist (Paice on the tambourine, sitting on a stool near Gillan). Blackmore has maintained his new-found interest, experimenting with a range of country-inspired phrases. For the first time in the concert, the band seems to be enjoying itself.

'Child In Time'

This is one of the last official live recordings that contain this song. Although Glover told Paul Cashmere the reason for its future excision was that Gillan was having problems reaching the song's highs, Gillan told *Metal Magazine*'s Anders Tengner in 1993 that there was more to it:

> Going through the motions. It got to the point where it was all a song about screaming, and that's not what it was about.

Gillan also maintains that the meaning of this song has evolved over the years. Initially intended as a statement about the build-up of nuclear weapons and the concept of Mutually Assured Destruction, he says that after the Berlin

Wall came down only a couple of years before, Germans took it as a song of freedom, as they did with the following track, 'Anya'.

Lord leads off with just a little deviation from his 1970-opening keyboard work. Gillan delivers a tour de force vocal performance, not just for his screams (which start strong but don't always get to the original's almost impossible highs) but for his soulful, quiet delivery of the first verse. Blackmore equals Gillan's commitment with yet another group of improvised full-speed solos. Paice gives an almost jazz interpretation of the rhythm, making it all a masterful display that could well be the definitive version of this emotive song of protest. Gillan caps it off with a line about seasons changing and all things returning, a lovely conclusion that becomes the lead into 'Anya'.

'Anya' (Blackmore, Gillan, Glover, Lord)
Lord's synth begins softly before Blackmore delivers some guitar lines that sound like finger-picking but done with a plectrum. When the song's anthem charges in, the band gives a rollicking performance. There is the occasional timing mistake and bum note, but the synergy is strong, particularly some stop/start moments in the middle, and Gillan's final few notes are a great capstone.

'Speed King'
Opening with a classical line, the band soon gets into a full-pace version of this *In Rock* opener. Lord and Blackmore echo each other in a revolving round of on-the-spot riffs. Then, oddly, they both go into a version of 'Teddy Bears Picnic'. Suddenly, Blackmore breaks into a full-on opening of 'Burn'. Then, more oddly, Lord pipes the 'Sailor's Hornpipe' before things come together again for a full hormone ending. Another great piece of work if interrupted by a few moments of Lord and Blackmore madness.

'Smoke On The Water'
The success of the previous track continues with this solid take on their signature closer. Blackmore and Lord produce solos, with Blackmore's being the stronger. Gillan plays with the audience as they sing the chorus. After a quiet section, the band hammer back in a moment so strong that it's almost impossible to think the band are in mid-implosion. One can only wonder what was about to be said backstage, but for this moment, in front of the audience, all could not be better.

'Talk About Love' (Blackmore, Gillan, Glover) (DVD Bonus track)
This is a thin version of the song, played with some apathy, so no wonder it was left off the original CD release. Blackmore plays along with the band, but there's plenty missing. Lord and Blackmore do solos, but there is a hole in the timing at the end of the soloing. This is an uncharacteristically low-key performance of a song that should have been a highlight of the concert.

'Knocking At Your Back Door' (Blackmore, Gillan, Glover) (DVD Bonus track)
This is an interesting take on the reunion album's opener. Blackmore is either inventive or destructive here, throwing in some lines that are far away from his recorded version, pulling the rhythm during the verses, although when it comes time to solo, the guitarist is right on. But once that is over, he returns to playing what could be a different song (or songs), including funk (something he eschewed in the 1970s). In the video, Gillan looks like he's having a great time, although his later comments that Blackmore was trying to strand him could well apply here.

'The Battle Rages On' (Blackmore, Gillan, Glover) (DVD Bonus track)
This is a faithful rendition of the new album track, apart from quite a few added vocal histrionics, including some of the highest highs of the whole night. Blackmore sticks to his work on the studio version, which is no surprise since the original is so busy he doesn't have a lot of space for improvisation.

'Lazy' (Blackmore, Gillan, Glover) (DVD Bonus track)
This is a traditional DP jamming song, and that is exactly what it is here. Everyone gets a turn to solo, occasionally on top of each other. As on *In Rock*, Gillan's harmonica work is a highlight, jumping onto a Blackmore solo. After a false ending, the band comes in to finish the track.

'Space Truckin'' (Blackmore, Gillan, Glover) (DVD Bonus track)
Promising some rock and roll, the band head into another of their classics, but Blackmore seems more subdued here, allowing the choral runs to be carried by Lord and Glover. It doesn't last long, just one verse, before merging into the next song.

'Woman From Tokyo' (Blackmore, Gillan, Glover) (DVD Bonus track)
Blackmore lays back again on this song, playing some simple lines that don't match the energy of the rest of the band. Once again, Lord takes up the slack, putting his keyboard into hyperdrive as Blackmore continues his (relatively) soft play. This again leads into the following song, making the three songs into a mini medley.

'Paint It Black' (Mick Jagger, Keith Richards) (DVD Bonus track)
This Rolling Stones track is almost unrecognisable until the words come in. Blackmore does some more energetic work here for a short time before Lord improvises with an inventive solo that bears comparison to DP's early progressive years. It's propulsive and compelling. Blackmore has left by this time, but he returns at the very end.

Purpendicular (1996)

Personnel
Ian Gillan: vocals, harmonica
Steve Morse: guitars, backing vocals
Jon Lord: keyboards
Roger Glover: bass
Ian Paice: drums and percussion
Record label: RCA/BMG
Recorded at Greg Rike Productions, Florida, US, between February and October 1995
Produced by Roger Glover (credited as Deep Purple)
Release date: 17 February 1996 (UK), April 1996 (US)
Highest chart places: UK: 58, US: did not chart
Running time: 62:16

Album Facts

If there is an album that shows a band rejuvenated, this is it. After the interrupted gestation of *The Battle Rages On* and the rift that was recorded on *Come Hell Or High Water*, the group was at a low ebb, even before Blackmore walked out.

The inevitability of his leaving should have been foreseen. In his 1995 interview with Jerry Bloom, Blackmore spoke of long-held regrets about the 1984 reunion:

> Looking back, I probably shouldn't have made that move. I should have stayed with Rainbow because Joe [Lynn Turner] was singing really well.

People leave bands all the time, but in this case, the suddenness was extraordinary. He did it in the middle of *The Battle Rages On* tour with, the band believes, the expectation that the tour, and the band, would end right there. Neither did.

Joe Satriani agreed to fill in and the touring commitments were completed. At the tour's end, there were some discussions about shutting down the band. Jon Lord, in particular, was exhausted, and he started considering the other fish that he, too, had to fry. His most personal album, *Pictured Within,* was in his head, yet he couldn't devote his time to it, this touring band business being a 24-hour gig. However, calmer minds saw that it did not need to end there, and the band, Lord included, decided to carry on with a new guitarist. Satriani was the early and obvious pick to become the new Blackmore. And it looked likely to happen because during the tour, Satriani told *Metalstar*'s Thomas Zeltwanger he wanted to sign on as a permanent member:

> We have a very strange contract situation concerning the recording of new albums. Very complicating! But if the band wishes to keep me as a permanent member, this would be my biggest wish, too!

Those contract issues proved impossible to overcome, so the band decided to explore other guitarist options in a democratic way: everyone made a list of the guitarists they would like to approach. Gillan says only one name was on all their lists: the Ohio-born Dixie Dregs guitarist Steve Morse, who had been voted by readers of *Guitar Magazine* as Best Overall Guitarist five times. Morse told Alan Stout that although he was approached by Gillan initially, it was Glover who offered him the enticing pitch:

> He heard of the trio and all the Dregs stuff and thought it would be really interesting and weird to replace the guitar spot with somebody radically different than Ritchie so that they wouldn't be seen as trying to copy him. I thought it was a bold move. It made me like the band before I even knew them.

That said, Morse also told the author he wasn't sure about the band because he had never seen them live:

> I said, 'What if these guys suck and live off their name, you know? I don't want to be part of that.' And I'm sure they thought the same thing about me.

These qualms were dispelled at their first jam when, Morse says, everyone started smiling. Gillan told Mark Foster in 1996 that with Morse on board, Lord had been playing the best since before *Machine Head*. Morse told Matt Resnicoff in 1995 that part of this was because he and Lord had a special synergy:

> Jon Lord has incredible ears; he really listens to a soloist. Even on the first show, he would play chords based on the note he thought I was about to hit. It's strange. Without meaning to, I improvise more in this group than we did in the Dregs.

In this environment, there were so many ideas flying around in the studio that at a full hour, *Purpendicular* became the longest studio DP album to date by a good ten minutes. Yet there is not a wasted second. The band members, in their new freedom, explore many styles without fear of veto. On no previous DP album could the Celtic sit with the hard rock, the shuffle and the waltz. And for this reason, this is an album that divides the DP fandom, even if Glover calls the album perfect.

It is also lyrically different to what had gone before. Gillan told Croatian television that during the sessions, he had a writer's epiphany:

> Let's start being men instead of boys, so let's not just write about fast cars and loose women, as we used to, but let's start writing about the spirituality of things, the expressiveness of life as it is, as a mature person. As soon as we went through that door, everything became so much easier.

The controversy about its enormous style palette aside, this album would lay the groundwork for the three decades of stability and creativity to follow. This alone makes the fascinating and ebullient *Purpendicular* one of the most important albums in the reunion DP catalogue.

Album Cover

In a big departure, the reunion DP logo is gone, replaced by the band name in a lowercase inconsistent serif font. The album name is drawn in red across the top third with lines that are perpendicular to each other. Looking like some paint strokes on a purple canvas. This could be the first tentative dabs from a band that was feeling new. Colin Hart says the cover was a very expensive exercise, with designers crisscrossing the Atlantic just to finalise the look of the broken match on the front of the album. The rear is in the same vein, with the track listing almost indecipherable in the same red ink font used for the album name on the front.

The packaging is, for the first time, heavily designed for CD. The cover unfolds to a nine-square poster. On one side, on a purple background, are the lyrics and the cover. On the back are photos of the band members on a black background, all looking meaningfully serious, except Morse, who allows a small grin. In keeping with the perpendicular theme, the credits are in lines along the edge of the unfolded cover that turn 90 degrees to the right until it goes right around. This makes for a clever concept but makes the reading a rather drawn-out affair. Legibility is not a priority here.

The name itself could have a few meanings. It could be a 90-degree change of direction for the band or an inference of a more personal nature.

All tracks by Gillan, Glover, Lord, Morse and Paice (unless otherwise noted)

'Vavoom: Ted The Mechanic'

DP guitars have never chugged like this. Paice was to say this sound was important to the band, being the first taste of Steve Morse. The new vibe extends to Gillan, who feels comfortable enough to open this era with a story about a man he met in a strip club. The difference between this and his other true stories is that Gillan takes it deeper, injecting some of the man's homespun philosophies, weaving them in with the clever phraseology of a writer reborn, describing Ted intriguingly as 'big as a truck, fast as a door' before throwing in the cryptic 'what's that?', perhaps mirroring the bewilderment of the listener. But unlike the crude toilet humour of that other new era opener, 'Knocking At Your Back Door', these words bear repeated listening. It works because the imagery of a man, both loving and fed up with his responsibilities (Gillan himself perhaps), melds so well with the push of the guitar, the relentless, almost background hum of the bass and the lightness of Paice's snare. This is a great opener that gives no clue to the broad palette that was to follow. It isn't blistering in the tradition of 'Fireball' or 'Comin' Home', but it works a storm.

'Loosen My Strings'

Suddenly, we switch down to a masterful slow-mid tempo piece that is almost unclassifiable, being a bit blues and a bit slow hard rock. But it is not really a ballad, either. From the beautiful bridge guitar opening to Glover's counterpoint riff to Gillan's yearning singing, this has no counterpart in the DP catalogue. To call this a progressive song would ignore the tight structure that underlies everything going on here.

The lyrics are a puzzle, too, a clever puzzle, but a puzzle. It starts with Gillan describing himself after a typical rock star's night out:

Wake up in the morning
Get into bed
closing my eyes
I rest my head

From there, he seems to be asking his partner for forgiveness for what we never know. It ends with a baffling verse:

Grease on the handle and the tangles in my hair
They always seem to go together, I don't care

Musically, all five members get their chance, led by Paice's snare and China cymbal. When Morse gets his moments to solo, they don't feel like an allocated slot but rather a melding of the ways. DP has not sounded this unselfish for a long, long time. If you want to explain what Morse has brought to DP, play this.

'Soon Forgotten'

A piping organ intro leads us into a strident treatise on the nature of politics and human behaviours. I think. Gillan is in full obtuse mode once again, and lines like 'the warriors of the flat earth have become the tyrants of the globe' promise much but fly off into a lyrical souffle that could be no deeper than a conversation with someone about a relationship. Gillan delivers these lines in an unrecognisable, almost chant-like voice in a double/triple-tracked lower register. The music also fits this vibe with an Orwellian organ. It all ends with Lord slowly, joyfully tearing it all down with a slowing set of the opening notes, leaving the listener wondering what the hell that was all about.

It's hardly the most relaxing or listenable track. It's very interesting but unlike anything in the DP canon, before or since. There would be more envelope stretching to come.

'Sometimes I Feel Like Screaming'

This is a song of great contrasts that Morse told the author came together almost accidentally:

> That was just me working on an idea and luckily, Jon Lord said, 'Hey, do you want to work on that?' I said I was just doing that little exercise for playing melodies. By the end of the day, we had the framework for the song.

Gillan delivers his most personal DP lyrics since 'Pictures Of Home'. The sentiment is similar: he's on the road with his band, he's lonely and feels trapped. In 1973, he was able to escape by quitting the band. Nowadays, he has no intention of doing that; he is much happier but has a home and a child to miss.

He hangs the story on the most minor of things: a note from home delivered to his hotel room, but the concierge's English is so poor that the singer can barely read it, making his feeling of isolation complete. Gillan wallows and we start to wonder whether we are going into dirge territory. But we don't because the gentle Morse fingerwork that so inspired Lord ends suddenly, and it all slams, like a brick into a pond, into a loud litany of complaints about the music industry and its 'wide-eyed boys with their bags full of money'. It does, however, land on an approximation of optimism:

> Heaven wouldn't be so high I know
> if the times gone by hadn't been so low

Actually, not quite. The black dog returns almost immediately:

> Sometimes I feel like screaming
> close my eyes
> It's times like this
> my head goes down

In the context of the regenerated and upbeat band, the dourness still works because Gillan feels he can open his heart without fear of another band member slapping it down. In fact, the band supports him fully, with a gusto. Gillan's bandmates are clearly enjoying themselves, and if the public doesn't buy it, then that's just too bad. As it turns out, the US audience didn't buy the song when it was released as a single, despite guitarist Morse being one of America's favourite musical sons.

There is also a fabulous vocal moment when Gillan, getting to his heightened emotional state towards the end, lets out a series of crystal-clear screams, unlike anything of old, both heartfelt and touching.

'Cascades: I'm Not Your Lover'

Now that Gillan has got all that out of his system, DP gets back to a good old hard and fast rock breakup song. It's cleverly worded and occasionally a bit harsh, especially when the spurned lover demands more of the singer:

You really must be going now
By god, is that the time?
Let me put you out of my misery
They call it being cruel
to be kind

It's cruel, yes, but Gillan makes it light as if he's telling the story to a bunch of mates. Gillan's protests are punctuated by wails from Morse's guitar. Morse told Rei Nishimoto that he was also responsible for Lord's following organ solo:

> I programmed some effects for him. 'Cascades' has heavy organ and guitar lines like in the old days when Ritchie and Jon played a lot of triplet lines together.

This was chosen for the live setlist for the following tour. It's not a particular change of pace (the band has plenty of medium-fast songs in the repertoire), but it is a showcase for everyone concerned. It's also in a lower register than in a lot of the old DP stuff. So maybe it's something that kills several birds, being new, fast, a showcase, and easier to sing. And it's a great, oddly life-affirming piece of music despite the subject matter.

'The Aviator'

Although Lord had explored the Celtic folklore genre in his own records before, this music had been strictly off-limits for DP. Morse told the author that he was the one who brought this kind of tone to the table, but it didn't always succeed with the fans:

> It earned me a bunch of beers thrown from about the seventh row on our UK tour. There was a certain percentage of the fans who didn't want to see the band change in any way. I, on the other hand, thought this band has the musicality to be broader than Led Zeppelin. I thought, open up the horizons.

The band celebrated this palette-broadening by releasing this track as *Purpendicular*'s second single. Like the first one, it didn't chart, but it seems everyone had a knockout doing it, especially Paice. He told the author at a workshop in 1999 that he liked the style of this one. He'd rarely had the chance to do the type of drum roll he does here (his self-taught mastery of the snare was demonstrated on a drum clinic Paice co-hosted with Red Hot Chili Peppers drummer Chad Smith where Paice shows an amazed Smith a one-handed press roll).

There are medieval overtones of guitar-as-lute with synths-as-chorus, and Gillan's lyrics begin in that style:

Riding on the moonpath
in the silver of the night

The fragrance on the air
was of another time
I cried in all my innocence
you were dressed in white

Moonpaths, silver nights, white clothes. The listener might think we are moving into Loreena McKennitt territory. But then comes verse two, which has no shred of an ethereal 'Lady of Shallot' about it. Instead, Gillan bemoans, once again, news media, warmongers, violence and profiteers. Gillan sets it in the context of being a pilot flying over the top of all this, removed.

The track stands out from the album for its loveliness and, except for some of the lyrics, its joy of life. Although Morse would explore this style again, such as in 'Contact Lost' from the *Bananas* album, the band would not put out another song like this. It is a case of a parallel universe that DP chose not to revisit. They proved they could do it. Now move on.

'Rosa's Cantina'

Lord opens proceedings with a church feel, as if the organist is warming up as the congregation enters. And when it enters, Glover hits with a groovy bassline, changing the church instantly into a house of blue light. Morse joins in with some understated semi-funk strums, and this funk feel continues with Paice, who gives us a drum line worthy of The Meters' 'Funky Drummer'. When Gillan enters with his story about going to the tavern in the title, the music has become a masterclass in how to be extremely busy without getting in each other's way. Gillan's voice is appropriately understated, waiting a full two minutes before he and the rest of the band start to rise as you suspected they inevitably would. Lord hits a solo, which might've come from one of his 1960s sets, being spacey and cool. The harmonica has two solos; the first is one of Gillan's best because he doesn't just follow the melody of the song but rather challenges it. He really should do more of this.

It should also be noted that there's no recognisable verse, chorus, solo, verse or chorus progression, just a funky, groovy bit of interplay loaded with highlights. It is another song that would be played live a lot, a kind of reunion 'Lazy', a musician's piece, and a load of fun.

'A Castle Full Of Rascals'

Once again, Lord starts the song (five out of six it is now) with a multilayered bit of business that is at once gothic and classical. Contrasts abound, with Morse's solid riff and screaming notes, Paice's funk rhythm and a very earnest Gillan.

It's only when we get to the end of the track that we realise that there's been no hook. This is one of the tracks that doesn't aim for top 40 play; it's the result of the band trying anything it pleases. Sadly, the record company would soon change all that. And this kind of interference is just what the lyrics are about:

Garbaggio from the men in grey
Don't do this, you can't do that
What's the point, what's the matter, anyway
Fat cat's licking cream
Dirty business, hard and mean
Narrow eyes and hungry days
There's got to be a better way

It's not just record companies. Gillan mentions castles, parliament, ivory towers and the *Texas Chainsaw Massacre* (which he intriguingly pronounces as massa-cree), which could refer to America's incursion into the first Iraq War. The joy of his lyrics is that we probably will never know for sure, and he isn't about to do our interpreting for us.

'A Touch Away'

This is a tender moment and a song that is unambiguous about love and need. It was brought to the table by Morse, and he opens with the right touch with sensitive fingerpicking. Gillan delivers similarly, singing of simple passion about being in bed with a woman who could be a partner or 'shady lady from shady lane'. There is intimacy and love on the road, perhaps. Affair or not, it's a song that celebrates love with no strings. Gillan doesn't do a lot of love songs in DP (or elsewhere, for that matter), but this does show he is capable. He will do more on future albums, but few will be as heartfelt as this one.

'Hey Cisco'

Gillan returns to the Wild West (as he does again to a degree on the next track). *The Cisco Kid* was an American TV show about two Mexican heroes, Cisco and Pancho, who fight the baddies and always end up laughing without causing any serious harm to anyone. The series ran in the early 1950s when Gillan was a young schoolboy, and the song imagines the series' actors some years later, disappointingly reduced to opening shopping malls. In keeping with the adventure theme, an accented Paice snare drum stroke roll fades in like horses on the mesa, accompanied by some fine picking from Morse. Things soon get heavier (or the horses get faster) with double bass drums and equally athletic bass lines. Lord stays out of the way until he gets a short solo before a high-noon duel with Morse.

It's not a song that says much, but like the titular character, it shines muscularly before leaving us wanting more. At the time, Gillan claimed that this was one of his favourite DP songs.

'Somebody Stole My Guitar'

Gillan shines lyrically in this gruff retelling of a banal incident: the titular stealing of his own axe somewhere in America. The words are edgy, full of

Above: A band promotional shot from 1984. (*Drew Thompson*)

Below: Still a pub band despite the American Joe Lynn Turner (centre), 1991. (*from the collection of Joe Lynn Turner*)

Left: *Perfect Strangers* – the album that started a 40-year journey. The best of it shows what could have been. (*Polydor*)

Right: *Perfect Strangers Live* is a belated release that shows the band in all its reunion enthusiasm. (*Eagle Vision*)

Left: *The House Of Blue Light* is an album beset with trauma, saved in post-production by Gillan and Glover. (*Polydor*)

Right: The poorest production in the band's canon can be attributed to *Nobody's Perfect* – the name says it all. The single is the only saving grace. (*Polydor*)

Left: A bold experiment took place in the form of *Slaves & Masters*. A new singer and new style make for a good album that still divides fans. (*RCA*)

Right: The effective 'Love Conquers All' single is even less DP than *Slaves & Masters*. (*RCA*)

Promo shots of Gillan (above) and Paice (below) in 1984. (*Drew Thompson*)

1984 Promo shots of Blackmore (above) and Glover (below). (*Drew Thompson*)

Left: Jon Lord and Ritchie Blackmore in Vermont, US, in 1984. (*Colin Hart*)

Right: Roger Glover and Ian Gillan composing in Vermont, US, during the same time period. (*Colin Hart*)

Left: Blackmore entertaining his fans in 1984. (*Drew Thompson*)

Right: Christmas Carols in Vermont, US, in 1984. (*Colin Hart*)

Left: A shot from a 1984 band rehearsal in Bedford, UK. (*Drew Thompson*)

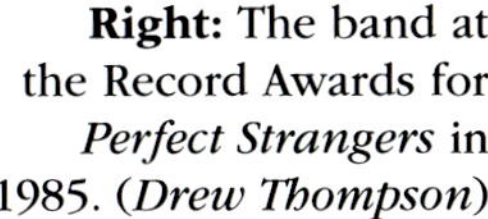

Right: The band at the Record Awards for *Perfect Strangers* in 1985. (*Drew Thompson*)

Left: *The Battle Rages On* – the last DP hurrah for an embittered Blackmore, but some moments are among DP's best. (*BMG*)

Right: Despite *Come Hell Or High Water* being a document of Blackmore's last days, it's surprisingly good for a band at its own throat. (*RCA/BMG*)

Left: A new guitarist rejuvenated the band on *Purpendicular* – a musical potpourri par excellence – but not all fans appreciated the experimentation. (*BMG*)

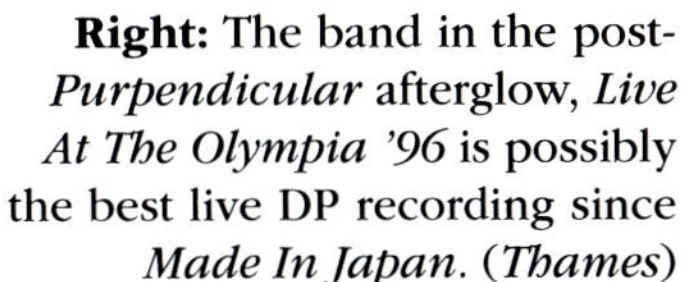

Right: The band in the post-*Purpendicular* afterglow, *Live At The Olympia '96* is possibly the best live DP recording since *Made In Japan*. (*Thames*)

Left: *Abandon* shows a return to DP's more rock roots, loaded with slow-rock, drum-led chutzpah. (*EMI*)

Right: *In Concert With The London Symphony Orchestra* – unfinished business from 1969 for Jon Lord, and this time, the band get into the vibe. (*Eagle*)

Above: *Purpendicular* days with Jon Lord in 1995. (*Drew Thompson*)

Below: The band in 2003. (*Drew Thompson*)

Right: The smiling Morse.
(*Drew Thompson*)

Below: Michael Bradford and Ian Gillan on stage.
(*Drew Thompson*)

Left: *Live At The NEC* showcases Lord's last hurrah and Airey's first. DP with two keyboardists makes for a triumphant night. (*BMG*)

Right: *Bananas* was the first studio album without Lord – it's a shaky start. A relative chart success belies the fact that it's not a great album. (*EMI*)

Left: Airey takes charge and DP get back in the swing on *Rapture Of The Deep*. (*Edel*)

Right: *Live At Montreux 2006* features Airey's first live recording without Lord. It's a reasonable job, but we've been to most of these places before. (*Eagle*)

Left: *Now What?!* is a strong offering and was dedicated to the former keyboardist they love. (*earMusic*)

Right: *Infinite* was a step up, both creatively and in sales. Bob Ezrin makes his mark. (*earMusic*)

Left: *Whoosh!* is the last album of original music with Steve Morse. Reflective and pensive, it has plenty to say about life and the future. (*earMusic*)

Right: *Turning To Crime* is a covers album that goes in every direction without pulling itself apart. (*earMusic*)

Left: A new guitarist makes his mark on *=1*. It's as rejuvenating an album as *Purpendicular*, but this time staying strictly Deep Purple. (*earMusic*)

Above: Too late: a 2022 *Whoosh!* tour shot with Steve Morse instead of Simon McBride.

Below: Roger Glover and Simon McBride having fun in 2023. (*deeppurple.com*)

Above: Looking up with eyes of devotion. Ian Gillan and his fans in 2023. (*deeppurple.com*)

Left: Multiple McBrides on stage in 2023. (*deeppurple.com*)

half-finished sentences that flit between sassy barmaids, booze, loud music, lonely old mountain men, threats of violence and theft. His evocative words are exemplified by this description of a bad night out:

The night is gettin' later
My head is gettin' lighter
The mood is gettin' darker
Tequila's being poured

The song also shows Gillan's stream-of-consciousness skill in this one-sided conversation, which sounds almost like a dialogue, which, of course, it isn't:

It wasn't long before
the waitress came over and said
Can I freshen up your drink
and have you heard of these boys
and if you feel inclined
to buy some cowboy boots
Well, it's not that bad
If you talk above the noise

Paice chooses a rare cowbell to give the song a more Western feel. Morse, meanwhile, is everywhere, with a wall of sound that Phil Spector would have loved. Lord again gets a short solo, which is not really a solo but more of a series of held notes that fit so well, before he banters riffs with Morse again. Nothing intricate, nothing surprising, but validation of the old line that less is more. It is an experimental track of apparently conflicting activities, yet it comes together miraculously in, despite the subject matter, a joyful effusion. Life affirmed.

'The Purpendicular Waltz'
The album finishes with a slow-mid tempo 3/4 chug about how it's all a pretty crappy life of odds. A harmonica opens proceedings before Morse gives us his very heaviest guitar, once again punctuated by screaming wails as if his axe is emoting Gillan's sentiments, until Lord, Morse and Gillan's harmonica compete in what could be a mess in lesser hands. They each hold their ground and end the album with a statement of intent. For a DP fan who has despaired of the band's misery in recent years, this is a hell of a moment in a hell of a song.

'Don't Hold Your Breath' (Expanded Edition bonus)
This extra track could be a garage band jam. Except, of course, that when DP jams, they are never going to sound like ordinary mortals. However, the words could have been made up on the spot, as could the solos.

It starts almost like a children's verse and quickly turns into a rough mid-tempo rocker. Strangely, this is the closest to a radio-friendly track produced by the *Purpendicular* sessions, with a strong hook and impelling rhythm. At times, the inventiveness runs out and it begins to mirror the rhythm, guitar work and synth of 'Somebody Stole My Guitar'. Thus, it's understandable why it was left off the first release of the album. As fun as it is, it just isn't up to the rest of the tracks from these sessions.

Live At The Olympia (1996)

Personnel
Ian Gillan: vocals
Steve Morse: guitars
Jon Lord: keyboards
Roger Glover: bass
Ian Paice: drums and percussion
Vincent Chavagnac, Eric Mula, Christian Fourquet: horns
Record label: EMI
Recorded at The Olympia, Paris, France on 17 June 1996
Mixed by Peter Deneberg, Acme Studios, Mamaroneck, NY, US
Release date: June 1997
Highest chart places: Germany: 98, UK: 183
Running time: 122.40

Album Facts

This live album was seminal in the history of the band, being the first live recording of the Morse era with the sanction of the Deep Purple organisation. It followed the twin live nightmares of its predecessors: the second-rate production of *Nobody's Perfect* and then *Come Hell Or High Water*, which could never be divorced from its onstage antics.

If *Purpendicular* was the album that saw the band fall in love with itself again, *Live At The Olympia '96* presents the band sharing this love with its audience. It is a jaunty album full of risk-taking musicianship. That it is a recording of a single concert instead of an amalgam of two or three shows that this DP was a confident band, playing at their best and doing it consistently.

Album Cover

Based on a concept by Roger Glover, graphic artist Jamie Webster created a graffiti graphic that somehow feels suitable for a live album. The band and album names are spray-painted with different fonts over a decrepit wall. Webster has painted the band name in the same way it was presented on *Purpendicular*, in a mix of bracketing and apparently random sizes with a dot before the last three letters, so as to make it a web address. Inside the booklet, the name is on a wall which has an eye painted on it, and the venue name is on another wall. Band photos abound inside. Many of the photos were provided by fans, some of whom are named.

It is a cover that doesn't take itself too seriously, and as the many smiles in the photos suggest, the intention of the whole cover is fun, almost bootleg. The rubble on the ground on the front cover might give a sense of decay, but the album itself suggests very much the opposite.

All tracks by Blackmore, Gillan, Glover, Lord and Paice (unless otherwise noted)

'Fireball'

On one of the most powerful numbers in the DP canon, Morse sets his own early stamp over the driving double bass drum line while Lord layers further with renewed gusto. The ending is intriguing, appending the first few bars of 'Into The Fire' from *In Rock*. The audience loved the reference, and one wishes the band had gone through with the entire song, but over the following 30 years, they rarely will.

'Maybe I'm A Leo'

A slow, funky drum intro leads into a laconic version of this *Machine Head* track. Gillan rarely reaches the recorded version's special notes and, early on, doesn't try. Everyone plays with aplomb; Lord changes the track's feel with a simple piano solo, and Morse throws everything he can into it, but it's all to no avail. This version doesn't match the original's verve; Morse's great work aside, this can be considered one of the album's few (relatively) ordinary offerings. A step back after the first track.

'Ted The Mechanic' (Gillan, Glover, Lord, Morse, Paice)

Things get energetic again with this rendition of *Purpendicular*'s opener. Coming so soon after the song's studio recording, it's not surprising that this is similar in most ways. Gillan's also back in business, hitting the extremes, particularly in the energetic and athletic last verse, where he stretches wonderfully.

'Pictures Of Home'

As red-blooded as 'Maybe I'm A Leo' was anaemic, this could be the definitive live version of this song. Morse and Lord squeeze out a tag-team synergy, and both drummer and bassist get their chance to shine, Paice on his fabulous opening sequence and perfect drum roll later in, and Glover on a rare bass solo run. Old has met new and it is a joyful reunion.

'Black Night'

We segue directly into this piece, which is played like the pop song it was crafted to be. Another tight rendition, but the pleasure is in what is between the notes: the band members throw in little bits of business and, for the second time in two songs, Glover ventures a few runs. The mix includes the audience's singing of the main melody. This is a fun decision, but it can get a little distracting, annoying perhaps, on repeated listening. There is a lovely bit of guitar and drum work just after the halfway point, followed by Morse playing with the audience, which answers his improvised riffs with surprising accuracy.

'Cascades: I'm Not Your Lover' (Gillan, Glover, Lord, Morse, Paice)

This newie begins just like the album version, which is amazing, considering Morse has to handle multiple guitar parts, especially since this is a slightly faster take. The only one who struggles to keep up with the new speed is

Gillan, who has to omit a word here or there. The second half is a slower exchange of apparently extemporary guitar and keyboard work that builds into an all-band jam session to finish the song, which, at 11.04, is the second-longest on the album.

'Sometimes I Feel Like Screaming' (Gillan, Glover, Lord, Morse, Paice)
Things slow down with *Purpendicular*'s most personal song. After a Gillan explanation about its genesis, Morse leads into the claps of the audience, which unfortunately handcuff the timing of the first part, but the band soon manages to take charge again. The vocals don't quite capture the pathos of the recorded version, but apart from that, it is a close rendition of a song that has Morse as its centre. His solos are superb variations of the originals, and he juggles several guitar parts very well yet again.

'Woman From Tokyo'
Morse switches immediately into a big riff from the past and does it with eerie fidelity to Blackmore's 1973 work. Gillan's on-off vocal work is back to its best and Lord's lively piano lays a solid bed for Morse, who breaks with Blackmore for the final soloing. Gillan adds in a bit of flourish, screaming his way through the song's final section behind the guitar and keyboard work, making this a great interpretation of a classic.

'No One Came'
Gillan gets in a playful mood for one of his most fun lyrics. Morse feels no need to stick to Blackmore's work for this *Fireball* track. Twenty-five years on from its studio recording, Gillan adds a bit of life experience into this rendition, singing it with a generous slab of cynicism and an occasional laugh. It's a brilliant example of how his perspective as a 50-year-old man can add depth to what was already an incisive piece of work. The last third differs significantly from the 1971 version, with the drums tougher and the guitar transcendent. In a 1996 interview with Dennis Karlsson, Glover cites this track as emblematic of the band's transformation:

> 'No One Came' was one of the big surprises. It became a fantastic live number. And it's refreshing, it's a renewal, it's the new Deep Purple.

'The Purpendicular Waltz' (Gillan, Glover, Lord, Morse, Paice)
The playfulness stops here. Gillan's harmonica starts on this, the final *Purpendicular* track and its cynical reflection on life. Gillan leaves off a few of his words (preparing his harmonica for its short solo, perhaps? If so, this should have been better organised). It ends suddenly, which is unfortunate because this offers a great variation of time signature and feel from the songs around it. Morse and Lord would probably have loved the chance to play with this a bit, but it was not to be.

'Rosa's Cantina' (Gillan, Glover, Lord, Morse, Paice)

The second CD opens with another track from *Purpendicular* after a quick Gillan introduction about a pub called 'The Witch's Legs' (which allows him to have a running gag across the show about the said legs opening and closing). This monologue is punctuated by shouts from the largely French audience, who may or may not have understood his innuendo. No matter; they were having a great time.

Once again, this live rendition follows closely to the recently recorded version, including a note-for-note bass and guitar intro, and the drum sound matches the original. Then Gillan misses his opening cue. Then he does it again twice more. Just when it seemed Gillan was not all that invested, he roars back with a great harmonica break and scat towards the end before another very good harmonica break to close things out. Even when hot and cold, Gillan can deliver.

'Smoke On The Water'

Gillan introduces this as 'one from Steve', and it soon becomes apparent what he means, with Morse going into one of his early Rolodex of guitar sounds as if he is flipping through past songs. Then he lands on this song's famous riff. Gillan sings it so sprightly; it's as if he's never done it before. This is not the most inventive of songs, but Morse pulls everyone into the mood and spurs this into something quite magnificent. The false ending at around 6.00 is no ending at all, just a lead into a Lord section which includes motifs from the song's story about the burning of the Montreux casino, including a fire truck siren, before going into a piano part that is classical, honky and comedic, before drifting it out to a softer close.

'When A Blind Man Cries'

The unusual close of the previous track somehow melds well into this song, also from the *Machine Head* sessions. It was left off that album because Blackmore didn't like it. Band members, particularly Paice, had long considered this omission a bad decision, so after Blackmore left, they would take to including this on their live setlist and rework it to make it into as much a guitarist's piece as a singer's ballad. Gillan sings just fine, playing with the phrasing and, in the process, giving echoes of his rendition of 'Gethsemane' from 1970's *Jesus Christ Superstar*. And for DP fans who were being introduced to Morse for the first time, his work on this piece explains just why he was chosen to fill the vacancy left by Blackmore.

'Speed King'

Ballad over, the band goes back into attack mode (after a soft intro), and in the apparent chaos is perfect control. Gillan once again loses words here and there, and it's to the credit of the band that they don't try to cover this up in post-production. It moves on from here to become something of a plaything for the organ and guitar, with Lord and Morse playing off each other over an extended section before a Morse solo. Gillan sings against Morse's runs, as he used to so do well with Blackmore before their relationship soured. There are a lot of ebbs and flows over its 11.46 (though the last two minutes are nothing more than Gillan's repeated thanks, applause and audience chats), and it is more proof that the band has new life. It's great to hear Gillan do the very high laughs of the original as if the intervening 27 years had not changed a thing.

'Perfect Strangers'
The band leaves, then returns to the stage not to do a series of oldies, but just one from the 70s and two from the reunion era. This one is as heavy as 'Speed King' was furious and is a great choice for an encore. The audience singing along proves that this 1984 single was already considered a classic. Only a few Morse screamers distinguish it from the work of Blackmore, and Morse's enthusiasm extends to Lord, who starts going to places he has not gone before in this song.

'Hey Cisco' (Gillan, Glover, Lord, Morse, Paice)
Gillan starts this by explaining that this gig is in the middle of a long tour before mentioning black & white TV, which is a quick reference to the origins of this song. Paice rides his fast double bass drum, which, at the end of a long concert, is quite a feat. A tiring Gillan hits some extraordinary notes and throws in some extemporary words that more than make up for a few missed words. This playful album track has translated well to a party tune perfect for the (almost) finish of a live performance.

'Highway Star'
The concert was always going to end with this classic from *Machine Head*, and the audience seems to know what's coming, some calling for it as Gillan hands over to Glover to introduce the three horn players who have been accompanying the band (if much of their contribution has been low in the mix). As Glover speaks, Gillan goes offstage and Glover gets playful, pretending not to give the singer his microphone back, as Paice begins this song's drum pattern. The audience is treated to the horn players doing a fabulous set of accents in the choruses, and Morse's ability to infuse his own take on Blackmore's solo work (without losing the power of the studio recording) is never more evident than here. When it ends, the audience sounds as exhausted as the band before chanting the players off the stage in triumph.

Abandon (1998)

Personnel
Ian Gillan: vocals
Steve Morse: guitars
Jon Lord: keyboards
Roger Glover: bass
Ian Paice: drums and percussion
Record label: EMI
Recorded at Greg Rike Productions, Florida, US, between September 1997 and February 1998
Produced by Deep Purple/Roger Glover
Release date: 2 June 1998
Highest chart places: UK: 76, US: did not chart
Running time: 56:18

Album Facts

If *Purpendicular* was an exploration of whatever style that came to their minds, *Abandon* harnesses that creativity into something closer to what their traditional fans might expect. Morse told the author that this album was not a conscious reaction to the first record, but it was framed in the understanding that some fans were not happy about *Purpendicular*'s experimental songs. That meant no Celtic tracks, no westerns, no waltzes.

One thing the band wanted unchanged from *Purpendicular* was that album's expansive sound, so they returned to the same unassuming little video studio in Orlando, Florida, hoping lightning would strike twice. It did. The tone was sharp, and the natural ambience shone through once more. So it might be surprising that Paice told *Modern Drummer*'s Adam Budofsky in 1998 that he was never completely happy with his sound on this album:

> A drummer sometimes has to just swallow his pride and go, 'Well, that's as good as I can get it.' It has a nice sound. I'm not putting it down. But there's always another 10% you could have found.

Despite his misgivings, his drums do come across as mighty. Part of that is the space Glover (as bassist and producer) gives him.

There is a freneticism, too, with their feet to the floor for a lot of it. This works for the most part, but there are places where they try too hard, like in the ballad (which doesn't match the one on *Purpendicular*), but overall, the album grooves a treat. Gillan shines here, too, his songwriting-as-commentary and autobiographical work being highlights.

The album was a mixed commercial success, though. *Purpendicular* charted higher in the UK, and neither that nor this album touched the US top 100. Maybe all this adjusting to an end-of-the-century audience was becoming a hard job for five men trying to be rock stars at this stage in their lives. They might need to have a rethink the next time they enter the studio.

And where did the name come from? Anyone's guess. Hints were dropped that it meant a band on the road and a band in total abandon, but no one has owned up to the answer definitively. It seems everyone was happy with the name, and that was that.

This would be Glover's last album as producer, and although they didn't know it at the time, it would also be the last to feature the full-time presence of Jon Lord, who told the author in 2002 that he was getting sick of playing 'Smoke on the Water' and had his own, much more personal music to do. With *Abandon,* he leaves the band well served.

Album Cover

This is yet another departure. Where the front of *Purpendicular* had simplicity at its heart, Abandon is the opposite. A skinny man in briefs dives from the top of a building to what must be a certain death. But that's probably not the message the band was trying to convey. More likely, it's about a feeling of freedom. Flying without a net, as it were. Maybe that's the point: he dives but never dies. He is just in a state of abandonment. Even so, it's a mysterious and oddly unsettling image that is repeated throughout the CD booklet with various angles on the death dive. Reflections of the landscape are shown in the building he is falling past. Ioannis (Vivid Images) designed the cover and booklet, which has no shots of the band itself. The booklet here is straightforward and easy to read, certainly compared to its origami predecessor. But it is all still rather odd.

All tracks by Gillan, Glover, Lord, Morse and Paice (unless otherwise noted)

'Any Fule Kno That'

If 'Ted The Mechanic' on the previous album was something of a departure for DP openers, the band goes one step further with this one. Owing something in the style of a rap song, Gillan's dense words charge across the top of his bandmates so fast that on first hearing, the listener has no hope of understanding what he's on about. What he's on about is greed and incompetence, particularly with the music business. In an interview on the *Total Abandon '99* DVD, Gillan says his disdain was heightened when he was told Joe Satriani was dumped by his label while on a sold-out world tour. This led Gillan to call the industry 'moronica', the epithet making its way into the lyrics. It's not all doom, however. The language, style and strident set of lyrics finish by expressing hope of a kind. There is even a tongue-in-cheek reference to one of his pre-reunion successes, 'No Laughing In Heaven', but you need a lyric sheet to pick that one up.

The music is just as interesting, starting off with a great drumbeat backed by Lord's undercurrent and Morse's riff that is both grinding and pulsing. The chorus is simple, just a Morse trill and the song title, before returning to Gillan's rap. The change after the second chorus is really interesting, with Gillan going higher:

> Won't it be nice
> When everything falls into place

And so, for DP, it seems that it has. Paice, in his usually understated style, considered the song 'wonderfully creative'. Hear hear.

'Almost Human'

Morse goes tough from the get-go on this brutal number. Lord plays second fiddle again to the many-tracked guitar and might've been wondering what he's doing here. He is there, bubbling underneath all along anonymously before finally getting a solo at the end, but not for the first time, it fades just as he starts doing some interesting work. Despite the familiar pace and riff, this track is unlike any they had done before. It has a series of changes that take it far from the realm of chorus/verse/chorus. Each change is a fascinating development, being presaged by a vocal lift.

As a single, it worked well enough for American audiences, reaching number 25 on the Rock Heritage Chart, making it the last DP single to reach the US top 100 for several decades.

Gillan told audiences in the 1999 tour that the song is simply about getting blotto in a pub and waking up the next day feeling like the title of the song. The lyrics suggest something more transactionally sexual to help cope with life on the road. Obviously, a few beers and a game of darts isn't enough.

'Don't Make Me Happy'

An odd love song, one that exhilarates and, at times, disappoints. When Gillan has gone the full balladeer, he's either done it with humour ('Anyone's Daughter'; 'Living Wreck'*)* or a genuine gentleness ('A Touch Away', 'When A Blind Man Cries'). In these verses, he does neither, his words uncharacteristically crammed into the music. Perhaps it's Lord's funeral dirge underneath that gives it a sense of enforced melancholy.

Then we get to the chorus, and it transforms. We hear a stunning performance from the Gillan we know, honest and demanding.

That said, where 'Almost Human' broke the mould for structure, this one takes us firmly back into verse/chorus territory, with a guitar solo after every chorus, leaving us with a song of parts, great and ordinary. But mostly ordinary.

'Seventh Heaven'

A guitar/synth/bass intro promises something tender and then, quick as a whip, we get into the closest DP gets to mid-tempo metal grunge. Morse again leads a series of intriguing changes, but the most interesting idea is to have the grunge drop out as Gillan sings.

What he sings about is his good fortune, no more, no less. And that good fortune is Morse. Gillan says this song was dedicated to Steve Morse, and he admitted to Czech journalist Ilja Kucera that the band didn't let the guitarist know this until after it was recorded because of Morse's natural shyness.

The rest of the band takes up Gillan's vibe. There's a quiet solo spot where Morse plays over a funky rhythm groove, with Lord supplying the backing, proving you don't need to lead to succeed. This is a band song of the *Purpendicular* kind: experimental, progressive, mean, but somehow touching.

At the last minute is an extra surprise: the return of Gillan's extreme wail.

'Watching The Sky'

Now, this is an interesting inversion of DP's usual soft start to a raucous song. The band charge in with a gunfire opening, which soon reduces into an almost zen section as Gillan claims to be doing nothing really, sitting by a wall, thinking. His gaze moves from the wall in the first verse to the passing water in the second verse and finally to the sky. There seems to be some theme about letting go of things. If he is referring to the band, then he could be taking us back to his 1973 resignation:

> I left my luggage at the station
> Didn't know how to say goodbye
> I walked away from all the fury
> And the madness and the fury

It is all so simple and repetitive that it might be a piss-take. The rest of the lyrics could be just an intentional load of gobbledegook.

> No matter, no matter, what's a man going to do
> One two buckle my shoe
> Zip my lip

If it is gobbledegook, it is beautifully framed gobbledegook, backed by a masterful score which surprises with its tight flips from heavy-as-can-be to gentlenes.

'Fingers To The Bone'

Another autobiographical song, this time couched in the terms of a farmer being put off their land. Thematically, it joins the previous track. Where that one may have been about Gillan's leaving the band voluntarily in 1973, this one is about his firing from the same band in 1989. As such, it is a song of disappointment:

Always been this way
It's the poor man who gets hurt
All you ever work for
Is to leave your footprints in the dirt

Gillan puts in a heartfelt performance. By the time he gets to the climatic last verse, he is almost crying:

And that's the way ill wind blows
You've got thirty days to pack your bags
Say goodbye, hit the road

His emotion is remarkable, given that he is singing of an event that happened a decade before, which was (as he admits in his autobiography) of his own making and has now been resolved with his re-acceptance by the same band members.

Lord plays contrasting piano runs underneath the chorus with remarkable lightness. Given that this is his last full album with the band, we get a glimpse of where he will head when he has his freedom.

'Jack Ruby'

Opening with a solid, semi-funk drum riff, Paice is joined by a so-fast guitar that suggests full-tilt fare is to come. It doesn't. Just as quickly as the guitar enters, it all falls back as Gillan starts singing.

His subject, Jack Ruby, was the man who shot dead Lee Harvey Oswald, who had assassinated US President John Kennedy in Dallas, Texas, in 1963. Ruby charged through a group of reporters in a police station basement to fire a shot into Oswald's belly a few days after Kennedy's death.

The song is not about Oswald, Kennedy or Ruby as such. Gillan sings here about having the verve and the nerve to do something as outrageous as Ruby's murderous act:

There's no method in my madness, no craft, no guile
No expertise, no self-assuring smile
No wizardry or witchcraft, no crass deceit
No dark conspiracies, I stand on my own two feet
I'm coming through just like Jack Ruby

Gillan, who has in the previous two songs gone through a resignation and a firing, talks about kowtowing to no one. Talking about it in terms of a murderer is a bold choice, although it strongly reinforces the message he's trying to make.

I don't beg forgiveness, I don't beg at all
But I beg to differ cos I got the ball

He could be speaking for the whole band because they sound like they mean business, every one of them. Lord sounds charged; Paice plays on point; Morse moves between double and half speeds and delivers one of his best solos; Glover allows himself to put his bass on top of the rhythm.

The album speeds and heavies from this point. They continue to be tight, but there's something about the space they give themselves on this track. From this point on, they never sound quite as euphoric as they do here.

'She Was'

As heavy as anything the band had done in years, Morse's guitar and Lord's synths work together to slam into the listener, while Paice displays amazing patience and is never tempted to drum into orbit. He gets a chance to cut loose, but only a little, as the band heads into the final chorus.

The words are not in the league of the others on the album. It touches on a woman who is desirable but emotionally closed, coming from the viewpoint of a man who appears to be heading towards jealousy. And that's it. Perhaps a throwaway, but one with a blockbuster vibe.

'Whatsername'

Continuing the theme of the anonymous sensual woman, this is an extension of 'She Was'. In fact, the two songs could have made an interesting medley. The woman in this song takes the emotional inability of the woman in the previous song one step further. She leaves the protagonist and then returns to do more damage.

Yet another long fade up (surely Glover and co. would have seen the sameness of the consecutive introductions) leads into a Morse riff that is remarkably like several we've heard before on the album, but the solos, samey or not, define this song. Morse's is followed by an organ solo, followed by another from Morse before Lord does another one, all of which are close to superb. There is also the easily overlooked gem of a guitar progression 40 seconds from the end where Morse's work sounds almost unrecognisable, more like Queen's Brian May than the axeman from a premier heavy rock band.

''69'

A soft guitar start belies the thunderstorm to come. We have already heard Morse's heavy, fast riff interspersed with an occasional screaming high note quite a bit, but it works well here, especially in the context of the lyrics, which take the listener back to the very early Vanilla Fudge-DP on the cusp of turning into the-loudest-band-in-the-world-DP.

The pace is not completely frantic. Just under halfway through, it all stops and heavies again with such tension between all the instruments that it feels as if the song is speeding up, which, of course, Paice would never allow. This is the last power track Jon Lord will ever do, and it's a beauty.

The lyrics are hard to follow (the singing is that fast), but they tell an inside story of those days from a man who was right in the middle of it all, just as he had done on 'Hungry Daze'. Again, we're in 1969, but this time, things are not looking so good. This is Gillan's version of AC/DC's 'It's A Long Way To The Top', complete with the fights, the due paying and the drinking. The lyrics are clever, with plenty of subtext. It all ends with some subtle references to the songs that were emblematic of the previous version of DP: 'Hallelujah' and 'Hush'.

1969 sounds like a hellishly great time.

'Evil Louie'

Gillan's social commentary song. Like 'Strangeways' and 'Castle Full Of Rascals' before it, 'Evil Louie' touches on bad behaviour among the elite. However, 'Evil Louie' is not an angry song. If it had been written post-9/11, you could think it was about that. But the World Trade Center was still three years away. The theme here is difference, which he slightly hamfists into the choice between fast food and cordon bleu. The point is still made, though, and there is an optimism that is missing from his previous political songs. The world is perfect, he says. The world moves on, and there's nothing any corrupt politician or anyone else is going to do to ruin it.

The music is heavy with a slow, tough bent led by Lord, Glover and Morse in tight unison on a grafting, crawling series of chords.

This is the last new track on the album, and it would have been a solid note to finish on. But someone had other ideas.

'Bludsucker' (Blackmore, Gillan, Glover, Lord, Paice)

Taking a song that you put out in younger days and revisiting it a quarter of a century later is a risk. 'Bludsucker' is a rerecording of 'Bloodsucker' from 1970's *In Rock*. The question is, why? Simply put, it was played live and got a good audience reaction. Morse told the author he thought it was a good choice for a retro tune. The truth is more likely that they thought it would be fun. Obviously, changing the name slightly was part of this fun.

You might think this revisiting would only work if you tried a different approach, perhaps one that reflects your more mature worldview. That's not what happens here. The band takes 'Bloodsucker' and does it again with minimal changes: The sound is fuller than the original, which was bass-heavy and had reduced a lot of the keyboards and guitar in the verses. Morse does add a little spice to the guitar work, particularly in the solo, and trades blows with Lord; whereas the last verse in the original has the singer scatting nonsense, in this version, he corrects this with real words. He also takes it up a notch, making it one of the most vocally challenging passages of the reunion DP catalogue.

Although they didn't know it at the time, this would effectively be Lord's farewell track, and as such, it works on almost every level.

Deep Purple In Concert With The London Symphony Orchestra (2000)

Personnel
Ian Gillan: vocals
Steve Morse: guitars
Jon Lord: keyboards
Roger Glover: bass
Ian Paice: drums and percussion
London Symphony Orchestra (Paul Mann: conductor)
Aitch McRobbie: vocals
Margo Buchanan: vocals
Pete Brown: vocals
Mario Argandona: vocals
Sam Brown: vocals
Miller Anderson: vocals
Ronnie James Dio: vocals
Graham Preskett: violin
Steve Morris: guitar
Eddie Hardin: piano
The Kick Horns: brass
Dave LaRue: bass
Van Domaine: drums
Record label: Eagle
Recorded at Royal Albert Hall, London, UK, on 25 and 26 September 1999
Produced by Deep Purple
Release date: 8 February 2000
Highest chart places: Germany: 32, US: did not chart
Running time: 127:22

Album Facts

This album represented unfinished business for Jon Lord. Having just released his most personal album, *Pictured Within,* Lord was planning further solo work. In this context, any thought of redoing his divisive 1969 *Concerto For Group And Orchestra* was furthest from his mind, especially as its score had been lost for many years, a loss that Lord says in this album's liner notes weighed on him.

The genesis of this concert came when Gillan suggested to Lord that he'd like to revisit the concerto. Lord was surprised, given Gillan's opposition to the 1969 production. But there was the issue of the lost manuscript. Then, as if by serendipity, Dutch composer Marco de Goeij approached Lord at a concert, saying he had rescored the concerto by listening to and watching the 1969 performance. With the help of conductor Paul Mann (who happened to be the nephew of DP's stage manager Colin Hart and was suggested by Hart), the score was completed, and almost exactly 30 years after the original performance, the band returned to the Royal Albert Hall (minus Blackmore of course) to recreate the concerto with the London Symphony Orchestra.

It was decided to make this into a bigger event than the original. Each DP band member would be given the chance to play some of their own compositions, inviting guest artists along. Across more than two hours on each of two consecutive nights, the musicians played these songs, followed by the concerto and then four DP numbers. The original plan was that the concerto would open the evening and then the band numbers would take the second half, but this was switched during rehearsals.

Colin Hart describes the concerts as 'a beast to put together' if just for the logistics of accommodating and transporting so many musicians. The emotional load was just as heavy. Lord told the author in 2002 that the preparation was stressful:

> It was full of tension because I wanted it to be so right and so good. The fact that it was being recorded and filmed. It was a lot to take on board.

The concerts became quite an event in the music industry. Among the audience were many stars, with George Harrison being one of a group having VIP status backstage. This intense industry focus and the resultant pressures seemed to drive everyone to deliver the performances of their lives, and at the end of the two nights, Lord's unfinished business seemed finished.

There was more to come, though. Just over a decade later, Lord would oversee a full studio recording of these concertos, which would be released shortly after his death in July 2012.

The recordings of the Albert Hall concerts were released on both CD and DVD. Neither rated strongly and only hit the charts (mildly) in a couple of European countries, but the band would play the concertos on a short tour, including in South America and Europe, with Paul Mann still conducting but often with a different orchestra for each country. This made DP's usual massive touring undertaking into something monumental.

Album Cover

This is a cover that says it all simply. In tones of deep purple, the cover by graphic designer Squalis shows a drawing of the Royal Albert Hall with a large whitish moon sitting atop the hall's dome, with a starry sky that continues around the back of the cover. In the hall's forecourt is a grid, which seems to serve no purpose except to draw focus to the image of the hall itself. The moon features on each of the booklet's double pages, along with photos of the band and Paul Mann performing at the concert and a composite image of the guest performers. It is a classy cover that speaks of both DP and the intensity of the performances.

All tracks by Gillan, Glover, Lord, Paice and Morse (unless otherwise noted)

'Pictured Within' (Lord)
This being a Lord-inspired project, it's apt that it begins with two tracks from Lord's recently released album, *Pictured Within*. Both are tracks made for the strings and both are highlights of the concert. This first song is Lord's most personal, canvassing his love of his family and life. His piano is aptly beautiful (as it is on the studio album) and Miller Anderson reprises his baritone vocal, which, with its deep tones, could not be more of a contrast to Gillan. This track also shows that this was no *Nobody's Perfect*; this live recording is going to be quite something in the DP canon.

'Wait A While' (Lord, Sam Brown)
English singer Sam Brown takes the lead on this second Lord track. She sings her own lyrics with as much aplomb as Anderson. The strings, particularly the cellos, are subtle for the most part but are felt more strongly in the second half of the piece. It is a delicate few moments, and the execution is wonderful.

'Sitting In A Dream' (Glover)
Then comes this Glover song, sung by Ronnie James Dio, who reprises his vocal from the 1974 concept album *The Butterfly Ball And The Grasshopper's Feast*. In a way, this is Glover's own 'Pictured Within', which is reflective and heavy on piano, strings and brass. The intricate score is understated while somehow managing to introduce us to the raucousness to come.

'Love Is All' (Glover, Eddie Hardin)
And when the raucousness does come, it's not in hard rock, but in this horn-driven anthem, the second instalment from Glover's album, again with Dio on the vocals. The sentiments about loving one's neighbours might seem a trifle twee so many years on from its 1970s origin, but in the context of the night and the event, it is appropriate. The circus middle section owes more to *Sgt Pepper* than to anything by DP, but the orchestra again fits the music, turning the song into something close to an anthem of love.

'Via Miami' (Gillan, Glover)
It's now Gillan's turn, and he chooses a track from *Accidentally On Purpose,* the therapeutic album he recorded with Roger Glover when things were going belly up for DP in the late 1980s. It is not the strongest track from that album, nor the most interesting, but it rips along. It is so fast here that Gillan appears to be having a hard time singing the relentless titular refrain. One wonders why he didn't do something from the more experimental albums from The Ian Gillan Band, such as *Clear Air Turbulence*, which would have been wonderful with a full orchestra. It must be said, though, that the brass section is a hoot.

'That's Why God Is Singing The Blues' (Dave Corbett)
Gillan's second choice is not a song of his own at all but a cover. It's a strange choice, but at least it gives some royalties to the writer, his good friend. The horns work well, and the words hint at the environmental and philosophical tangent Gillan would take on some later DP albums. Still, lyrics about the world 'turning into a dying zoo' and suchlike is a bit of a downer on this celebratory night. Confusing guitarists Steve Morse and Steve Morris is an amusing mistake, more amusing for his attempt to correct it.

'Take It Off The Top' (Morse)
For Steve Morse's turn, he plays his own heavy progressive track, one that Morse told the author was badly received when his band Dixie Dregs released it in the UK years before (he remembers one review simply saying: 'Take it Off…Please'). It leads off with a riff that is very close to the opening of 'House Of Pain' off the upcoming DP album *Bananas*. His own band (bassist Dave LaRue and drummer Van Domaine) back Morse, with the horns and the violin solos augmenting perfectly. Perhaps more than on the concertos themselves, this is one of the album's most effective blends of the heavy with the orchestral.

'Wring That Neck' (Blackmore, Simper, Paice, Lord)
Another instrumental, a jazz-fusion number dating from 1968's *The Book Of Taliesyn,* was a groovy, well-recorded number back then. Here, it comes into its own, and it was presumably Paice's choice for the concert since it is a showcase for his drumming and was his first named co-writing credit. While his drumming was good on the original, here he goes the full Gene Krupa, syncopating and soloing unleashed. The end is all his, despite the video revealing he lost a stick in the middle of the closing solo, somehow managing to snatch it back. The horns also star, having been given a new arrangement, which makes the song something that would have sat proudly on any jazz-fusion record of the previous 30 years. Another highlight of the night and a surprise for any listener who had thought DP was just that 'Smoke On The Water' band.

'Pictures Of Home' (Blackmore, Gillan, Glover, Lord, Paice)
Again, this is probably a Paice choice, for it is a showcase of his skills, particularly the breakneck opening. On *Machine Head,* he starts it alone, but here, the orchestra opens for him, making the drum break into the song proper more surprising. The song may be a drummer's piece, but its majesty lies in Gillan's words about the loneliness of being a rock star on the road. The orchestra is mostly heard in the song's accents, but the rest of the time, it is subsumed by DP's members, who all solo, including Glover (who gets two). This leads into one of the sequencing oddities of the album, where Gillan introduces 'Ted The Mechanic', which comes after the concerto. That should

have been picked up, but then again, it could simply have been a Gillan mistake on the night.

'Concerto For Group And Orchestra Movement I' (Lord)

So much has been said over the years about the three movements in Lord's concerto, many of them negative. The author remembers a classicist telling him in the 1970s that it was not a particularly good concerto. If compared to Mozart, this is perhaps accurate, but this was certainly not the view of conductor Paul Mann and, before him, in 1969, Malcolm Arnold. In this first movement, which Lord named by its tempo and style, 'Moderato-Allegro', the soft woodwind opening leads to strings which bring us earthbound. The string plucking section gives a percussive contrast, leading into a yearning sunrise moment that is very Vivaldi. Playful moments follow, and one can almost see children frolicking. Up to this point, it is not an orchestra-band fusion; it's been purely orchestral. Then, at 7.00, the band enters, taking the movement into something far more rigorous. Morse's guitar takes a lead break, followed by a bass line and a guitar solo. Soon, the orchestra knits in with the band, giving the group-and-orchestra concept its raison de'être. Each band member plays off the orchestra, leading to the sublime confluence of band and brass at 11.20. The movement revisits some of the earlier refrains, this time with a woodwind section, before the drums return, accenting in perfect synchronisation with the tympani before a strong closure.

'Concerto For Group And Orchestra Movement II' (Music: Lord, Lyrics: Gillan)

This movement, 'Andante', begins quietly, the woodwind and strings interplaying in a way that is as unsettling as the first movement's Vivaldi-influenced section is calming. Then, at just over four minutes in, Lord introduces the motif for the movement, a motif that will be taken up by the singer, who brings in questions about life and its contradictions. The lyric may have been written by Gillan in a rush in 1969, but here, they take on a truth that might have been less certain on the original recording when his success and its excesses were still in his future. The movement then goes into one of its loveliest sections, melding contemplation nicely into Gillan's words. It is interesting how well the band works with the orchestra; the organ slowly replaces the strings at around 10.30, almost without the listener realising it. Morse hits with a gorgeous rock and blues solo before Gillan returns to further his lyrical musing. He is not called on to stretch his voice, and correctly so, for his screams would have been out of place here. The strings tag-team with him, echoing his melody, and it works better than in 1969. Morse hints at a guitar solo, which has all the pathos of the words. Then, Lord takes charge again, his organ leading the listener into a much more hopeful and upbeat part before a sublime final contemplative section. This movement is much longer than the other two, at almost 20 minutes, but it has switched so many times that it feels much shorter.

'Concerto For Group And Orchestra Movement III' (Lord)

This piece, dubbed 'Vivace-Presto' by Lord, is where the concept of a concerto for group and orchestra works best. Brass and percussion give a strong opening into strings that are evocative of open spaces. A restrained section takes the listener out of this realm into something far more complex. Morse is so at home with the orchestra that it's no wonder he was asked back to do the studio recording 12 years later. Strangely, Lord's organ is not quite as successful; the listener is instantly aware that we are now back to the band, but this is only for a moment. Paice gets a drum solo, but it is so well placed that one cannot tell when the orchestra's drummer finishes and Paice begins. The orchestra's percussionists take over again and drive the movement, with Paice augmenting. This is a complex piece of music that finishes the concerto with verve and imagination. Wow, says Gillan, before adding they finally got it right. Too true.

'Ted The Mechanic'

Morse goes from concerto to a fast and incendiary slam of an intro. As the song gets underway, the brass adds accents, and although it's fun, it's not really necessary. If there is any track in this concert where the guitar should have been left alone to shine, it is this.

'Watching The Sky'

The same could not be said of this power song, which could have been made for orchestra right from the dynamic opening, which leaves space for backfill. Sally Herbert's orchestral arrangement is simply stunning, heightening what is already a dynamic piece of work. She would provide equally powerful augmentations on the next two songs.

'Sometimes I Feel Like Screaming'

Judging by the audience's reaction, Gillan's patter going into this song must be witty, but it is mixed so that he can barely be heard. The orchestra arrangement starts in the less-is-more vein, with the strings rather dormant before going big for the underlining of his line 'I see your face'. In the strident chorus, they pull and push Gillan, adding to the feeling of dismay inherent in the lyrics. Being a personal song, though, the backing vocals don't quite sit right despite being well delivered. Gillan didn't need them. One element that comes out in this version is Lord's piano, which, while mixed behind Gillan in the softer sections, contrasts with the increasing orchestrations. It's a fascinating rendition that, once again, successfully mixes group and orchestra, if a little busily.

'Smoke On The Water' (Blackmore, Gillan, Glover, Lord, Paice)

The obvious end song, and one where everyone, including the guest rock players, joins in. Dio sings the second verse, showing his difference in style to

Gillan. They share duties on the chorus, as do the backing singers (and the mixing in of the audience singing the chant). Gillan returns for the third verse and seems to have been inspired by Dio, for he throws everything into it and succeeds. Morse hits every note he can in his solo and ends it with a homage to Blackmore in a slow set of notes over the top of the returning riff, which is a magnificent blend of keyboards, horns and orchestra.

Deep Purple Live At The NEC (2008)

Personnel
Ian Gillan: vocals, congas
Jon Lord: keyboards
Ian Paice: drums
Roger Glover: bass
Steve Morse: guitars
Don Airey: keyboards
Record label: Eagle
Recorded at Birmingham NEC, Birmingham, UK, on 2 September 2002
Produced by Deep Purple
Release date: 2008
Highest chart places: UK: did not chart, US: did not chart
Running time: 134.00

Album Facts

At the Albert Hall concertos, the only remaining members from DP's 1968 inception were Lord and Paice. Now, it was to be only Paice. Lord's 2002 announcement that he was leaving the band caused some surprise in the industry but not within the group. Glover told Rasmus Heide in 2003 that he had seen the writing on the wall as Lord withdrew more and more from the others, especially on tour:

> There was a feeling on the Concerto tour that made me think Jon was going to leave at the end of that tour. It had obviously been on his mind. Ever since *Pictured Within,* it seemed obvious that his mind was really more focused on orchestral music.

On his website, Lord said the decision was inevitable, but it wasn't easy:

> By 2001, I was beginning to lose sleep, going around and around with the thought that I couldn't see how to make both things run parallel; that is, to stay in Deep Purple and yet have the time to concentrate on and write the kind of music that was more and more in my heart.

And that kind of music was released two years later in *Beyond The Notes*, which could not have been more different to DP, with cellos, choirs and the occasional birdsong. It even has Lord on the cover holding a conductor's baton.

With Lord now gone to this new musical life, there was a chance the band he founded would fall apart. Morse confirmed to the author that he, too, considered leaving at this time:

> I was going through a tumultuous time personally, and the band represented my security. But the magic and the communication during the

first album and early tours with him were absolutely the peak of my time with the group. I just loved the way he [Lord] would try my suggestions and always have logical alternatives if he didn't agree and smile while playing along if he did agree.

Morse did decide to stay, and part of this was probably due to the signing of keyboardist Don Airey. A bandmate of Glover's in Rainbow, Airey had filled in for Lord well on an earlier tour after Morse had joined the band.

After Airey accepted the gig, the band tried something new, a live onstage passing of the baton between the keyboard players, with Airey doing half the concert and Lord the other, the idea being to allow Lord to farewell his DP fans. This meant that, for the first time, Lord had to listen to his own group from backstage while waiting to go on. Lord would say it was a strange experience that caused him some complex emotions.

There were other emotions as well. An altercation involving someone in the band camp and a cameraman saw the camera crew go on an instant strike. The DVD's executive producer, Drew Thompson, who had been in the recording van outside the venue, told the author he managed to smooth things over, although the origins of the disagreement were never discovered. Remarkably, the fracas did not make its way onto the music, which was warm and engaging throughout.

The song list is interesting for being top-heavy with songs from the Blackmore era (including some more obscure numbers) and for 'Hush', a song Gillan said they should not have recorded for *Nobody's Perfect*.

Airey and Lord had been sceptical about the dual keyboard concept but believed it worked out well in the end, particularly in the encores.

And it did, both as a band event and as a concert. It is a bit sad that it failed to chart on either side of the Atlantic.

Album Cover

This is the epitome of simplicity, with individual shots of all the band members, including both Lord and Airey. The text font suits the live aspect of the recording, with the band and concert names printed as if on the side of a road case. There is a deep purple haze, or blurred images perhaps, behind the photos. The sleeve notes on the back tell the story of the night. It's all functional but clear. It should be noted that this is the only time that a non-compilation DP album has six band members listed.

All tracks by Blackmore, Gillan, Glover, Lord and Paice (unless otherwise noted)

'Fireball'

Another new era dawns with a new look. Gillan has shortened his tresses and is wearing a new stage getup: an all-white kaftan over baggy pants and bare feet (a uniform that crew members thought was kind of weird). The song proves a good opener for Airey because the keyboardist delivers a solo that pays homage to Lord's original but with enough of a difference to show he is the new guy. Glover does a killer solo, too.

'Woman From Tokyo'
Airey shows his classical chops as Gillan flexes his considerable range. One can only wonder how long he can do it, but so far, it's been so good. It may be a straight rock number, but the band, particularly Airey, demonstrate their individual prowess across this simple beat.

'Mary Long'
With Blackmore gone, the band go into this 1973 parody of two British wowsers, Mary Whitehouse and Lord Longford, who, as Gillan tells the audience, made the band's life difficult. He says they are 'up there' and 'not laughing', a gentle cross-reference to his non-DP song 'No Laughing In Heaven'. 'Mary Long' is a strange choice because its groove is a little pedestrian and its lyrics are wordy. It may have been Gillan's favourite, but no one else in the band has owned up to similar feelings. This arrangement jazzes it up a bit with a guitar break, but the whole piece lacks the energy of the rest of the set. It's not for the lack of trying. It's just the number.

'Ted The Mechanic' (Gillan, Glover, Lord, Morse, Paice)
Four tracks in and we finally get the post-reunion DP. This rendition nails the studio version, new keyboardist and all. It's just as wordy as the track before it, but Gillan acts the words, almost taking you into the pub where the story originated. At the very end, Gillan claims that the character's real name wasn't Ted; it was Martin, and he wasn't a mechanic but a wine merchant. He then admits Martin the Wine Merchant didn't scan very well. Fabulous guitar solo, by the way.

'Lazy'
This *Machine Head* blues classic was always a Lord play piece, and it is the same for new boy Airey, who uses the introduction to riff into a range of eras and styles, including Lord's rather overplayed 'Sailor's Hornpipe' motif. Then they get down to business, with Morse stealing some of the keyboard intro. But this is Airey's showcase, and he throws everything at it.

'The Well Dressed Guitar'
Gillan introduces this as a new track that has not yet been recorded for the upcoming album. It would not make it onto the record, and it should have because it is grandiose in its interplay between the keyboard and guitar. It could have been an anthem if Gillan had sorted out how to fit words over the top. Short and gorgeous.

'When A Blind Man Cries'

Another song vetoed for years by Blackmore, so there's an irony that it's the guitar that makes this work, particularly in its sensitive intro. Morse only very occasionally lets the moment go to his head when he lets his fingers play with maybe a touch too much busyness for the moment.

'Space Truckin''

Staying in the *Machine Head* era, Morse and Paice's intro is complex and a huge contrast to the simple riff that starts the song proper. Airey fills the background in sync with Glover's runs which are near as dammit to the original. Morse, again, is faster and busier than Blackmore, but just like the studio version, Paice proves just what cracking a drummer he can be. Even Gillan laughs at how good he is.

'Keyboard Solo' (Airey, Bach, Beethoven, Mozart)

This is Airey's first chance to shine on his own and he does it by starting with Bach's 'Toccata' before taking us into a classical music journey through a medley that contains a snippet of Beethoven's 'Ode To Joy' and Mozart's 'Sonata No.11'. Things then get sci-fi with John Williams' 'Star Wars Main Theme', followed by crashing thunder. Suddenly, the lights go black.

'Perfect Strangers' (Blackmore, Gillan, Glover)

When the lights come up, the crowd is ecstatic to see Jon Lord on the same keyboards. He leads into this definitive latter-day organ showcase. The band lay back slightly, allowing Lord to have one of his last times in the DP sun. A touching few minutes it is and, along with the time George Harrison joined them onstage, one of the band's live highlights. Lord stays on for the next few songs, although at this stage, no mention is made of Lord or Airey, let alone the handover between the two. The audience knows.

'Speed King'

This begins with what Gillan would call a bit of Morse skiffle. It's over in a few seconds, and the band crashes into this heavy staple. It is busy but is not the semi-metal song it is on *In Rock*. Here, it's about trading licks between Lord and Morse as the rest of the band lays down the beat. At one point, Morse goes over to Lord, and the two musicians clasp hands mid-song as Glover begins a rare extended bass solo that becomes a distorted grunge. Paice then has his moment, going into fast rolls. It is virtuosic but threatens to outstay its welcome as he finishes, restarts and stops suddenly, to the apparent surprise of his bandmates. Also surprising is Gillan leading into Boyd Bennett's 'High School Hop', which is, nevertheless, a good excuse for a bit of guitar, vocal and piano improvisation. Then comes Elvis Presley's 'It's Now Or Never', Roy Orbison's 'Dream Baby' and Ray Charles' 'What I'd Say' before going back into 'Speed King', only this time heavier and truer to the 1970 recording. All in all, quite a trip.

'Guitar Solo' (Morse)

After all the classical and rock roots revisiting of the last few minutes, we lead into yet more time travel with Morse, who takes us only as far back as the 1960s with a snatch of Lynyrd Skynyrd's 'Sweet Home Alabama' before going into his musical Rolodex and coming out with The Who's 'Won't Get Fooled Again' and Led Zeppelin's 'Whole Lotta Love'. It's all somewhat improvised, with Morse signalling the changes to the rest of the band. He then surprises with a bit of Bach's 'Jesu Joy Of Man's Desiring'. Morse told the author that the Rolodex idea worked well, but after a while, the band got tired of it, so this is one of the last recorded examples of his trip through musical history.

'Smoke On The Water'

After Morse's intro, Lord is joined by Airey on keyboards, making this the first time two DP members played the same instrument. Gillan messes up the words in the first verse, throwing in bits from the second. He sees the humour of the fluff, flinging up his hands to the audience. He then joins the two keyboard players and sings the chorus with Airey. After the obligatory audience singalong, the band takes it out, led by the keyboards. In the end, Lord and Airey grip each other and shake hands. The baton is being passed.

'Hush' (Joe South)

Given this is Lord's final official appearance with the band, 'Hush' feels appropriate, given that it was the band's first hit, and so it allows Lord to give it his 1960s progressive treatment, backed solidly by Paice, the only other band member from those days. And doesn't Lord make the most of it in his several solo spots?

'Black Night'

As Lord swaps back to Airey, the repertoire goes back to the old favourites to take the night out, but not before Gillan throws in some of Gershwin's 'Summertime'. What follows is a surprisingly low-key delivery by the band. Well, it has been a long night. Morse plays his solo with Gillan behind him, thumping at his congas, which are, as usual, barely heard on the recording.

'Highway Star'

Lord is back with Airey, but it is Morse who takes the lead, simulating making love with his guitar (tastefully, though, if such a thing is possible). After stressing his voice early in the night, Gillan has been able to pace himself for these last moments.

Then that's it. All over. Lord comes to the front of the stage as the audience chants his name. He is hugged by the men with whom he has travelled so far and so long before going off to his new life.

Bananas (2003)

Personnel
Ian Gillan: vocals
Steve Morse: guitars
Don Airey: keyboards
Roger Glover: bass
Ian Paice: drums and percussion
Beth Hart: backing vocals
Michael Bradford: guitars
Paul Buckmaster: cello
Record label: EMI
Recorded at Royaltone Studios, Los Angeles, US, January and February 2003
Produced by Michael Bradford
Release date: 9 September 2003 (UK), 7 October 2003 (US)
Highest chart places: UK: 85, US: did not chart
Running time: 51:25

Album Facts

Five years is a long time between DP studio albums, but there were a few reasons for the long wait this time. *Abandon*'s lack of success was certainly a contributor, as was the concerto and the two-year world tour that followed, and then a US triple bill tour with Ted Nugent and Lynyrd Skynyrd. Jon Lord's departure, though, was the biggest impact (after he had already worked on two songs for the new album and played on one of the demos).

With studio time booked, Glover decided to hand over the production of the record to Michael Bradford, telling *Classic Rock* magazine's Paul Rees in 2018 that after producing every album since the reunion in 1984, the band had stopped listening to him. American Bradford had credentials. He had worked with Anita Baker and Madonna and, at 42, was considered a rising star in the record production world. Bradford had also played with DP briefly, filling in for Morse on a TV show in Europe, and the band were quite amused when this African American musician introduced himself to the TV audience as 'Ritchie Moreblack'. This on-stage synergy meant Bradford was considered a musical peer, and this led him to do more than just produce the band; he would co-write three of the songs and play guitar on one of them.

The result of the recording sessions was an album that experiments with styles, although nowhere as much, or as interestingly, as on *Purpendicular*. DP seemed to be after relevance and, at times, was talked into going where it probably should not have gone. The first single, 'Haunted', is an example of a track that would never have been recorded with Blackmore and probably not with Lord. If the song had charted, then the world may have seen a different DP evolve, but its failure meant the band would not stray so far again.

That said, this is not a poor album. In the light of the studio albums preceding and following it, *Bananas* could not be anything but overshadowed. The fact that no songs on this album remained on the touring setlist for long might also suggest the band felt the same way. However, the album did score some reasonable reviews and still charted in the UK, so Bradford was brought back for the next album, which would prove to be much more DP in nature.

The band followed up the new release with yet another tour, including a run across North America in February 2004 with a setlist that included the entire *Machine Head* album.

Album Cover

DP has always been a band that has put a lot of effort into its covers, from the Mt Rushmore of *In Rock* and the reflective metal of *Machine Head* to the red wine glass of *Come Taste The Band*. Sometimes, they tried too hard, like on the odd bauble effort of *Who Do We Think We Are*.

The *Bananas* cover goes the other way. Clearly, someone believed that a photo taken by the band's manager of a couple of banana reapers on a pile of bananas had the potential to be a classic. If the album it contained was a success, then maybe the image would have gone into pop culture history. As it is, the album's modest success did nothing for this banal cover. The shot breaks the cardinal photography sin: the focus is skewed, pulled to the reaper in the middle, not the bananas themselves. The bananas look like foliage, so that message is shot down. There are other distractions, like the beam across the top and the guy on the left who is half cut off and looks annoyed at the photographer's intrusion.

The back has an overhead image of a guy pushing a barrow of (still greenish) bananas. The gatefold edition at least has the bananas coloured right on the inside fold. There are a couple of band shots, a concert crowd, and some banana production photos, which again speak to nothing.

With this cover, the band offers a confusing, weird piece of artwork. It was not the best way of introducing a new member.

All tracks by Gillan, Glover, Airey, Morse and Paice (unless otherwise noted)

'House Of Pain' (Gillan/Bradford)

This is new. This track is not in the brutal class of the band's classic openers but is still solid rock, with some enthusiastically tough Morse guitar riffs. Gillan speaks to the listener directly, asking whether they have ever had a bad relationship before taking it into the first person and revealing he's in the same position and just can't let go. Neither the music nor the words take us anywhere, although there are some scintillating moments towards the end with some Gillan highs, bookended by some harmonica. Yes, as has been the case on so many of the recent albums, the interesting bits come at the end and fade out too early. The new producer, Bradford, should have listened closely to earlier DP work; he would have seen how the band traditionally started their albums with firecrackers. It's good, but just not that good. Note, too, that Gillan is the only band member given a writing credit.

'Sun Goes Down'

Things instantly get slower, with a layered Lord-ish synth introduction that builds suddenly into a showcase for both guitar and keyboard. Airey has fitted into the band so well that the changes are seamless. The vocals fit well with the backing, although the words are largely spoken.

The lyrics are personal, beginning with a line for his fans, who are 'looking up with hearts of devotion'. But it seems that even this adulation doesn't give the singer satisfaction with his life. Yes, it's another loneliness on the road song, but it's done well. The third stanza contains the gem in depression writing:

Let me tell you there's no point knocking
At the big oak door
Can't you see that it's all full up
They can't take no more
You know the line's so long
It's almost Disney
Ooh, won't somebody kiss me

This song is a masterpiece of layering: vocals, backing vocals, guitars and, mostly, Airey's keyboards. There's a scintillating double hit of two keyboard solos near the end, which announces that Airey is here and he's ready to muck in. This makes for an album highlight.

'Haunted'

Morse told the author that this song came from Glover, who was going through some personal turmoil at the time, and he expressed his emotions through the lyrics. It's true that they do fit the dourness of this kind of trauma:

I hear your footsteps on the ground
Tempting me to turn around
It's just the echo of a disenchanted lover
Shuffling aimlessly
Homeward bound

There are some lovely moments elsewhere in the words, but it does feel like everyone is trying a fraction too hard, perhaps doing it for Glover. After a soft guitar and keyboard intro, drums and vocals crash in, destroying the mood somewhat. Part of the problem is Gillan, who throws himself at it hook, line and everything else. Airey drops in some lovely piano towards the end, but the best part of the song is the guitar solo, which is touching in a Paul McCartney 'My Love' style, making it unlike any other in Morse's DP catalogue. The addition of Paul Buckmaster's strings shows a lot of investment was put into this piece.

This was chosen as the album's single, and its music video tried its best to show DP verité, laughing, travelling and clowning. Then, the last part of the clip goes black-and-white and shows the band performing live. The upbeat video bears zero correlation to the sense of the song it's promoting. The backing by American singer Beth Hart, as good as it is, only reinforces the song as contemporary MOR, a place DP has never ventured before and will never go again. It's no wonder it didn't chart in any major market.

'Razzle Dazzle'

For some reason, this is one of Gillan's five favourite DP songs. At the same time, the singer admits that Paice hates it. It's that kind of song. A nice enough, but hardly inspiring, backing gives Gillan a chance to talk about going out at night in the town. Obviously, it's a nod to the rock n' roll of the 1950s and Bill Haley's hit of the same name. But where 'Speed King' referenced Little Richard's hits 'Good Golly Miss Molly' and 'Tutti Frutti', they were wrapped in the hard rock that would define the new DP. This track does nothing of the sort. Even the terminology sounds of another era. If the band was aiming to connect with the youth of 2003, they were not going to do it by talking about going out on the razzle-dazzle, which is about as hip as seeing you later, alligator. The musical highlight is the inventive bass line, although Bradford puts it low in the mix. Airey throws in honky tonk piano, which puts a new complexion on something coming out under the DP banner. A slight song, nevertheless.

'Silver Tongue'

This is closer to the old DP. Even the normally self-effacing drummer says he produced a great rhythm. It's the last minute of the song that is the gem, when the band breaks out into a jam, including some scatting from Gillan, who once again gives us an on-the-road lyric, but instead of complaining about emptiness, eagles and snow, he seems to be saying that has come to terms with the touring life:

You know I can dream in any language
Flying in my magic bed
And I don't need to work my passage
Yeah, all I do is use my head

There's no great emotional insight on offer except to say that he is getting by, using his 'silver tongue', which in Gillan-speak could mean anything: his wits, his singing voice, or maybe something a little more personal.

'Walk On' (Gillan/Bradford)
A ballad that would like to be another 'When A Blind Man Cries' but doesn't approach it. After some synth work, Morse comes strumming, setting the song up as the solid ballad it never becomes. It's hard to put one's finger on why. There are certainly enough changes to keep the song interesting, including what seems to be a middle eight that turns out to be still part of the verse before the real middle eight comes in. All these additions are pleasant without being brilliant. The lyrics should be affecting, being an ultimatum to a disapproving lover:

If you don't like what you see
If you can do better than me
Walk on

The story even offers a little pathos as the protagonist goes belly up:

I won't hold you down
You need a little space

It's just that Gillan doesn't sing them with his usual conviction. It's hard to imagine a tear being shed by any listener, and for a song with this one's pretensions, this must be the sign of whether it succeeds.

'Picture Of Innocence' (Gillan, Glover, Morse, Lord, Paice)
Morse's funky guitar and Paice's equally Motown rhythm combine to give one of the album's more original openings. In fact, the pair had come up with the track when working alone together in the studio. Lord contributed to their initial fun.

Then comes the lyric, a co-write between Gillan and Glover. It was added much later, and it feels like it because it has little to do with the playfulness of what is running underneath. What we get is a diatribe against what one (or both of them) perceive as political correctness:

No drinks, no smokes
No dicking around
No dirty jokes
Straight lace, straight face
The old straight jacket
We got no hope

This is obviously personal because, further on, Gillan says he is so misunderstood. Stung by a few online comments, maybe? As the author of some of the 1980s' more audacious lyrics, including those about the ping pong woman Mitzi Dupree, Gillan had an attitude of 'shock them – who cares if they don't like it?' The 2003 Gillan seems to care now, and like a dad in a pub bewailing the loss of the Benny Hill days, Gillan defends dirty jokes and dicking around. Of course, it could just have been that the two friends, writing alone together, goaded each other until a complaint became an anti-woke rant. Either way, if 'Razzle Dazzle' made Gillan sound dated, then 'Picture Of Innocence' goes one step further by making him sound like a grumpy old fart.

It's unfortunate because under the diatribe is a fine piece of music. One wonders what the rest of the band felt about their music being so usurped. Was it a case, perhaps, of the lyricists having no clothes?

'I Got Your Number' (Gillan, Glover, Morse, Lord, Paice, Bradford)
Originally titled 'Up The Wall' when it was played live as an incomplete number with input from Lord, this finished version starts with a great drum groove from Paice that's ever so tight with the bass and guitar. And interestingly, it starts mid-bar. All too soon, this musical fire settles into being a backing track for Gillan to tell us about a relationship that is going bad. On the surface, it's a romantic theme, but knowing Gillan, it could be about past bandmates, politicians, wowsers or record company executives. Or maybe it's about nothing at all:

> It's that same old nonsense
> That same old look
> But now I'm turning back
> And I can read you like a book
> It all means nothing

Whatever the target, again, the words are less interesting than the music that backs it, although the soft break that comes at 2.18 sounds like it's going to offer something special but delivers little more than a heavily echoed Gillan stanza of a cryptic something-or-other. Airey, who hitherto has filled in the backing with nothing much, finally gets something to do with an organ solo.

In all, it is a tight, well-played song of very little importance. The definition of an album track.

'Never A Word'
This track reminds us of what can happen when the band tears out of the proverbial envelope. Airey and Morse lead into one of the more lovely DP ballads. Unlike on some earlier tracks, when Gillan joins, the synergy is maintained. The words are just as affecting and are delivered in an uncharacteristic Gillan gentleness. He stretches into his higher register for his personal love paean, and all this makes him sound more honest.

This is a band listening to each other. Paice offers little more than cymbal crashes and rimshots, and that is all that is needed. The bass is equally simple.

The album would have been better had there been more of this.

'Bananas'

After the progressiveness of the previous track, we return to the straight rock & roll that we have heard so much of earlier on the album, and it's not attacked in a particularly new way except for a novel 7/4 time signature, but this is not enough to make it anything but a sow's ear.

The opening is almost a copy of that of 'Walk On' with a sci-fi keyboard feel that has very little to do with what follows.

Gillan's words also start unpromisingly, confessing he has writer's block:

I've got nothing to say today
I used my words up yesterday
I'm just lying here in the sun
Watching you guys having fun

The band does sound like it is having fun, occasionally going off into a frenzy, particularly in the last quarter of the song. They are acting bananas, like the song's title.

After cleverly turning his lack of inspiration into a lyric about crafting a song, he engages in gobbledygook, which is probably meant to convey that he has also gone loco. But we never learn the relevance of the Alice that he's supping with. Or his mathematics degree. The strange thing is that everything is sung with conviction.

The guys may have been having fun, but it sounds too much like they are playing for themselves, not the listener.

'Doing It Tonight'

As we reach the close of the album, we get a piece with an engaging Paice rhythm.

Gillan's lyrics are of the bestial sex type, but the lust he feels is for someone who, as usual, is barely described. He sets the lyrical stage early when he sings: 'I imagine we'll be doing it tonight.'

This would seem straightforward, but as the song continues, these words change meaning from an expectation of sex into him fantasising about having the said sex. The way he uses the same words to convey the two meanings is rather clever.

There is also a smart rap section about halfway through. Airey's synth solo is a corker, too. In all, it is a celebratory piece of music that has the chutzpah of DP in its best times.

'Contact Lost' (Morse)

'Doing It Tonight' was going to be the closer, then a tragedy happened. In February 2003, the space shuttle Columbia broke up as it attempted to re-enter Earth's atmosphere. All seven crew were killed. American Steve Morse wanted to record a brief musical tribute to the shuttle's occupants, and this was put on the end of the album as a last word. It is the only DP track credited solely to Morse and the only wordless reunion DP track to that point.

The song would feature on tour for a short time. Gillan would sit on the stage floor and introduce the song before passing over to Morse. On the album, it is a touching afterthought for a mixed bag of the inventive, the autopilot and the derivative.

Rapture Of The Deep (2005)

Personnel
Ian Gillan: vocals
Steve Morse: guitars
Don Airey: keyboards
Roger Glover: bass
Ian Paice: drums
Record label: EDEL
Recorded at Chunky Style Studios, Los Angeles, US, between March and June 2005
Produced by Michael Bradford
Release date: 24 October 2005 (UK), 1 November 2005 (US)
Highest chart places: UK: 81, US: 43
Running time: 55:48

Album Facts

Although the previous album, *Bananas,* showed some chart success, the band was dropped by EMI. Any disappointment was short-lived, for they were quickly taken on by the German-based EDEL label and this gave the band impetus to go for a follow-up. They invited Michael Bradford back as producer and would record new material at his home studio. They also looked at some material that was left over from the *Bananas* sessions. With these connections to the past, one might expect this would be *Bananas Pt II*, but it is nothing of the kind. *Rapture Of The Deep* is an album with a pop-rock sensibility that the earlier album never had. It would also be the most successful DP album since Blackmore left, breaking into the US *Billboard* Independent album charts at 43. It also made the top ten in Germany and the top 20 across Scandinavia. In all, a slap in the face to EMI's A&R people, although part of the success must be due to the new label's heavy promotion of the product.

It is a long album, and several times towards the end, it starts to revert to the old tropes, but for most of its journey, this is a refreshing set with plenty of tracks that sounded great on the radio. Being the first album with no input from Jon Lord, Airey felt free to experiment throughout. We should note here that the Airey/Morse DP will prove to be the longest-lived version of the band, sticking it out for close to 20 years. It was not to be so for producer Bradford. Despite his relative success with the band, he would not produce another DP album.

Album Cover

After the oddness of the *Bananas* cover, this time around, Glover reunites with Ioannis (Vivid Images) to give us what could be seen as the logical sequel to the sleeve on Abandon. We have another single-man figure, but instead of jumping off a tall building, this man is pensive, watching his reflection in a pond of water. The image ties in with the name of the album, although there's not a lot of rapture on display. The image is sprinkled throughout the CD artwork and 16-page booklet. DP are aiming for a quality package here, quite the reverse of the album that came before. There are no cheesy band shots nor 1980s gatefold splotches of colour. This design is consistent and funky, although the purpose of all this is something that must remain in Glover's head. Note that there is an interesting reversal of the second 'e' in the band's name (every album seems to be an experiment in fonting the name). On the lower front is the album name in a relatively hard-to-read text, which is much lighter than the larger band's name at the top. Obviously, DP has decided it was more effective to trade on its name rather than the album title. It's a strangely satisfying cover, though, despite the fact that a flick through the booklet reveals there's not much to keep one occupied for more than a couple of minutes.

All tracks by Airey, Gillan, Paice, Glover and Morse (unless otherwise noted)

'Money Talks'

A bright start, courtesy of Airey's keyboards, develops into an industrial dirge of sounds (a full one minute's worth) joined by a Morse grind. It's a strong opening that suits the sentiment to follow.

The lyric begins as a Gillan confessional in the mode of 'Ted The Mechanic' from *Purpendicular*. The confession is about his younger, carefree DP days when money was no object. He takes us through his solo period when things became tight, and this singer business was no dream. Then comes a reversal: in this last third of his life, he has gone back to loving money again. If there is a point here, maybe it's that you only appreciate what you have once you've lost it. Or that he's just become a greedy old bugger.

The song is refreshingly new in its vocal and instrumental delivery, Gillan throwing in some surprising 'hoo-hoo' backup vocals. It's also nice to hear players all going for it, everyone but Airey that is, who is relegated to echoing the bass, filling in the background or doing some fills. Even when it comes to solo time, Morse gets two; Airey nil.

'Girls Like That'

A snappy number that is probably the most pop-oriented song offered by the band since the Joe Lynn Turner days.

The lyrics have smarts, but they haven't dated particularly well. Gillan sings about a phone fight with a significant other, where he claims the woman has misunderstood him to the point where he becomes a victim, putting it down to 'Women, yeah, being what they are'. But the lyrics are otherwise fun and self-deprecating:

She said you know what I mean
But I couldn't understand

Didn't know what she said
I'm a reasonable man

The punchline is a total reversal, where he claims to want girls who do just what this one has done to him. All this makes the song not a criticism but a eulogy.

The music is led by a speedy Morse riff doubled by Airey keyboards, which are used more effectively than on the previous track.

As on the first song, Gillan goes for screams (he also throws in the odd cheeky laugh). That he is in such obvious delight promises much for the rest of the album.

'Wrong Man'

Compared to the joy of the last track, this one is quite a bit more lyrically and sonically downbeat. The protagonist is in jail and accused of some unnamed crime. It's a simple story of a delusional criminal protesting his innocence, like in Gillan's much darker 'Sacre Bleu' from *Future Shock*.

Morse gives us his well-practised grind, and he does it relentlessly, except for some spots in the verse when he stops for Airey to pop in some answering keyboard. This guitar solo is a lesson in austerity and it's a lovely thing to hear. Paice beats a groove the band must've loved because they let it go on far too long, for after the last chorus, the story has been told and the music has given the listener everything. Glover claims that many of their songs begin as a jam, and it's a good bet that this is an example. It's not often that DP outlasts itself in a song, but it does here.

'Rapture Of The Deep'

This title number may be the most progressive on the album and one that Gillan likens to 'Pictures Of Home' in its inventiveness. Morse opens with a rather unsettling riff that morphs into the opposite, a calming slow-mid tempo funk groove, while Gillan sings about an ethereal place where he can do some lovin' and carin'.

Morse told the author the opening guitar riff owed more to Airey than himself because it was the type of scale that the keyboard player used a lot. But Gillan takes it from there, ramping up the tension before it returns to a love scenario. A listener might even conclude that the chorus sounds terribly like Gillan simulating an orgasm.

And that's what we have. A round of being told things are great, things are bad, things are better, then sex. Gillan gives us a day in the life with the point unclear. There is a line at the end that says this is the rapture of the deep. So it's about sex, then.

There are many twists and turns in this song that are worth listening for. There's a lovely moment just before the guitar and organ solo when Gillan scats along with the guitar refrain.

It's an unusual piece in that the earworm is the opening and closing riff, not a melody or a chorus. And it works as a memorable treat.

The band was proud of it. This was to be the only song on the album to be released as a single. The lack of chart success doesn't devalue it. This is not a traditional single. Then again, neither was 'Smoke On The Water', and look what happened there.

'Clearly Quite Absurd'

This lovely slow song has one of Gillan's finest lyrics. The reason it works so well is that aside from the smart words, there is honesty in how they are delivered, supported by a band who knows that the magic here is with the singer. They let him shine.

Gillan gives us a monologue from the viewpoint of a man who has just (yet again) had an argument with his nearest and dearest:

The turmoil and the conflict
You don't have to feel that way
Look into my eyes
And feel my hand upon your heart
Holding us together
Not tearing us apart

Yet there is no mansplaining or condescension. In fact, later in the song, Gillan comes as near as dammit to begging for a reconciliation.

It may be a singer's song, but there is acuity across the rest of the band. Paice uses little more than a snare and his ever-present China cymbal. Morse has a lovely slow set of trills, and Airey provides a wall of sound synth, some effective piano parts, a Hammond solo and (for some reason) some sci-fi effects near the end. But the medal still must go to Mr Gillan.

'Don't Let Go'

The pop centrepiece of the album, this starts like a jam, so much so that the drum sound is nowhere near as prepared as on the rest of the album. This contrasts with the clarity of Glover's compressed bass, while the keyboards stay relatively muted.

All that applies until we get to the chorus when Gillan's 'I said!' leads us into a hook on the song title that pulls in the whole band, especially the organ, which comes from nowhere to take the lead. This is a pushing, pulsating number that features no progressive moments. It's pure pop rock.

As for the lyric, we have already seen that girlfriends and arguments seem to be a Gillan obsession on this album. This is the third song on that theme, but here Gillan takes us back to the girlfriend argument of 'Girls Like That', using a few of the words on that earlier song to express his confusion about how things got this bad:

I can hear voices they're buzzing in my head
Eyebrows raised, was it something that I said?

Sounds like it. Elsewhere, Gillan gives us some of his oddly fascinating descriptive narrative:

A long hot night, it crept in like a thief
The engine stopped, the seatbelt popped
And her jaw dropped in disbelief

These could be the nimblest lines since he described Ted the Mechanic as 'big as a truck, fast as a door.'

Despite the downbeat topic, the song, like all good pop songs, is a great romp. It would have made a corker of a single.

'Back To Back'

A big change of vibe, led in by Paice on a relatively simple (for him) funk groove. It is soon overtaken by a guitar and synth riff.

This time, Gillan laments that the 'average man is uplifted five times a day', and in his autobiography, he explains that 'uplifted' is his euphemism for something more down-and-dirty, the statistic coming from an article found by his missus. From this start, Gillan sings his heart out on these lyrics as if they are Shakespeare, which, unfortunately, they're not:

I'm just begun
When you're all done
I see you running down the road
Can't hear a thing
My mind is blasted
And my head is about to explode

The chorus is the gem, though. While the words are just a few repeated lines – 'gotta use it, gonna lose it' – the rest of the band jams out on its straight-four funk with Paice playing piercing quarter notes on his cymbal bell interspersed by guitar and keyboard punctuations. For the second time in three songs, Airey throws in strange sounds that really don't mean anything at all in the context of the song or its lyrics. Never mind, nothing is going to make this lyrically pointless jam sound anything less than sublime.

'Kiss Tomorrow Goodbye'

A hard, angry song that puts a coming environmental apocalypse in terms of a good man who made a mistake, perhaps representing the whole polluting, emitting human race. Gillan's writing is not at his most subtle, nor is the song easy on the soul because the rest of the band are just brutal. A solid tom intro by Paice leads into heavy guitar chords that are probably the closest Morse has yet come to that Blackmore sound: hard and incisive. As are Airey's keyboards.

There is no chorus as such unless Gillan's repeated claims to have done the 'bad thing' qualify. There are solos, also angry, a return to Paice's jungle drums, and one more verse (yes, also angry) before Gillan tells us we have already run out of time:

The writing is big and it's there on the wall
Oh how the mighty empires fall
There's nothing to fix it's much too late
Sit down and prepare to meet your fate

This gives us a DP rocker that harks to the days when they were not afraid to let it all hang out.

'Junkyard Blues'

Although it doesn't feel like it, this blues is in almost the same tempo as the track that precedes it. There are plenty of changes, but it aspires to be nothing more than a great jam. That said, the change leading to the verse is a lovely thing, as is the New Orleans-style drum and bass pattern throughout. The false ending is also a surprise.

The sentiments in the words are like Paul McCartney's much more sedate 'Junk' from his 1970 solo album. Gillan describes a junkyard of rotting waste, although there is more to it. He doesn't just talk about the rubbish; there are drunks, relations (relatives?), bones and most significantly, home. Why would all this detritus remind him of home? No idea, but he's doing more than giving us a guided tour through the pollution underworld. The clue may come in the last lines of the last verse:

All this stuff was good for something
But here it is now, good for nothing

Is Gillan having doubts about his use-by date? Hope not.

'Before Time Began'

We finish with something else again. Taking the tempo down from that of 'Kiss Tomorrow Goodbye' and 'Junkyard Blues', this one succeeds in making a much stronger statement in a far gentler way. So soon after the invasions of Afghanistan and Iraq, Gillan (and probably the whole band) decide they cannot finish the album without making a plea for peace. To do this, Gillan tries a new method, delivering his lines in broken halves. He builds his power until the end of the second verse. By this time, you realise that Paice's rolls are not some Celtic style but rather something much more martial, building to Gillan's final plea:

Every day of my life I discover
Someone murdering my sisters and brothers
In the name of some god or another
What do you know?

The band immediately jumps into guitar and organ solos, which feels a little bit like a lost moment. When Gillan returns, it's with a much stronger repetition of the plea. And just when you think it's all about to end, Gillan gives us another verse, delivered in one of his most passionate tones. But before he leaves us, Gillan delivers one last spoken sentiment:

And for those who remain with your chosen gods
May your prayers be answered

This might sound a little hokey, but it must be remembered that this is a song of its time, when racial and religious difference was a topic of the moment. In 2005, it was most probably seen for what it was: a wish for unity in humanity.

'Before Time Began' gives us great work from the band, particularly Gillan, and the best ending on a reunion DP album since 'Hungry Daze'. It is also a portent to the introspective pleas that will come on later albums.

'Things I Never Said' (Japanese bonus)
A ripping live song that is headed by an almost instantaneous guitar solo followed by an organ solo, and then many more of the same. Obviously, it developed from a studio experiment that may well have been a chance to blow out the cobwebs because everyone gets too many chances to have a blow. It's as busy as can be, and for once, it seems that no one worries about trampling over each other, including the usually circumspect Glover. This is one of those few songs that the band loved to trot out for a live performance but would never envisage putting on an album. Good decision.

'MTV' (Special Tour Edition bonus)
A minor track with a half-hearted backing; it is easy to see why this was not put on the album proper. Yet Gillan put a lot of effort into this treatise on the lack of support in the broadcast media for the more mature rock bands. Gillan obviously needs to get this off his chest and does it very wittily, if a little bitterly. One highlight is his tongue-in-cheek reference to inept interviewers:

Mr Grover 'n' Mr Gillian
You musta made a million
The night that Frank Zappa caught on fire
Could you tell us all about it

Therapy songs have a place, but that place being on a major album is another thing. The invective, as clever as it is, just sounds bitter. The rest of the song is nothing particularly inspired. A worthy bonus track, but that's just about all.

Live At Montreux 2006 – They All Came Down To Montreux

Personnel
Ian Gillan: vocals
Steve Morse: guitars
Don Airey: keyboards
Roger Glover: bass
Ian Paice: drums and percussion
Record label: Eagle Rock
Recorded at Montreux, Switzerland, on 15 July 2006
Mixed by David Richards
Release date: 12 July 2007
Highest chart places: UK did not chart, US: did not chart
Running time: 67.33

Album Facts

Credited as the first official live release by the Airey incarnation of the band, *Live At Montreux 2006 – They All Came Down To Montreux* was recorded at the Auditorium Stravinski for the 40th Montreux Jazz Festival. Interestingly, its release came only a year after the similarly titled *Live At Montreux 1996,* which was a delayed release of a concert recording from the early Morse days (and with Lord still on the keyboards). That earlier album featured mostly songs from the 1970s, with only two reunion-era songs. Ten years on, the early hits still dominate, but there are four newer tracks, all from their most recent album, *Rapture Of The Deep*. Of course, 'Smoke On The Water' features on both albums, seeing as the concerts were held in the city of that song's story. While the 1996 recording reached the top 100 in Germany, this 2006 collection failed to chart in any other significant market, which is probably no surprise given the two albums were released so close together. The DVD version has an expanded setlist which includes 'Hush', 'Black Night', 'Well Dressed Guitar', and a jam which features the harmonica playing of Claude Nobs – described as 'Funky Claude' in the 'Smoke On The Water' lyrics – who rescued fans when the Montreux casino burnt down during that infamous Frank Zappa concert in 1972.

Album Cover

A break from the style of the live albums that surround it, this interesting design owes nothing to DP's studio album covers either. For a start, it is mostly white, with the only trace of purple being in the DP logo, which is a melded lowercase 'D' and 'P' that share their vertical stroke. There are strips along the album's top and bottom, each with four photos of the band playing live. The album name is in the same scribble script that adorned the 1996 Montreux live recording. The back is equally simple, with the same DP logo above the tracklist. It's not a particularly inventive cover, but it has a touch of class.

All tracks by Blackmore, Gillan, Glover, Lord and Paice (unless otherwise noted)

'Pictures Of Home'
Paice starts the concert with the same athletic four-limbed opening drum soloing that marked the studio recording. Gillan shreds his 60-year-old voice from the get-go, although he does miss some cues, possibly because of vocal overreach. It only lasts for a short time before melding into the next track.

'Things I Never Said' (Gillan, Morse, Glover, Airey, Paice)
This song from the recent recording sessions suits Gillan's voice much better, allowing him to talk/sing with aplomb. Glover lays down a groovy walking bassline that, in a rare occurrence, dominates Paice's drums. Morse's solo is accomplished but could be seen as a trifle overwrought, hitting every possible note and not letting up. Airey's organ solo is just as fast and frantic. So, what we have is an entertaining rendition of a minor song, just the sort of thing for a live performance.

'Strange Kind Of Woman'
There's no rest again before the band go into this concert regular. Gillan is in great form, playing with and stretching his phrasing, and his call and answers with Morse near the end are particularly fun. Morse's solo is a high point, completely different from Blackmore's work, and it shows, again, some extraordinary fretwork. The song is tougher than any of the earlier versions, and this change makes a very good song better.

'Rapture Of The Deep' (Gillan, Morse, Glover, Airey, Paice)
A new song at the time of the concert, this rendition sees Gillan singing with conviction, including his simulated orgasm at 1.30 (which gives the title of the song a new schoolboy suggestion). But once more, this is Morse's showcase, as he cuts loose on the song's progressiveness. On the record, he was a great player. Here, live, he is a virtuoso, running through a range of styles across the entire proceedings and nailing it every time.

'Wrong Man' (Gillan, Glover, Lord, Morse, Paice)
On this middle song of three from the new album, Gillan is in prime form. Everyone works hard, but it is almost as if the singer is taking up all the air in the song, and the others are happy to give it to him.

'Kiss Tomorrow Goodbye' (Gillan, Morse, Glover, Airey, Paice)
For the last *Rapture Of The Deep* song, there is no waiting around. Paice jumps into his tribal drum beat for this song about the future or lack of it.

Gillan again sings the lyrics as though it is indeed about life and death, but messes things up. He makes a mistake with the fourth line, confusing 'hole' and 'rock'. It would not have mattered, except he tries to correct himself a bit clumsily. He forgets the lyrics entirely in the second half of the second verse, but this time, he replaces the words with an extended growl, which, in the context of the song, works surprisingly well. The solos are largely anonymous (apart from a cool glissando from Airey), but the handover to Paice's outgoing tom rhythm is fabulously executed.

'When A Blind Man Cries'

Gillan again turns back time on this 1972 blues ballad, singing it with the same verve, and perhaps a bit more, than he did back in the day. Given the original's sorry gestation and blackballing by Blackmore, this might have made a great track for studio re-recording. Certainly, this remained a band favourite, having been on the setlist for many years.

'Lazy'

This song used to be the band's jam number in the 1970s, but in the early Morse days, it was kept relatively short. Here, it has been reinstated as a longish (7.34) playful, experimental number, just like it used to be. After doing a short homage to Jon Lord by throwing in, yet again, that trite 'Sailor's Hornpipe' riff, Airey plays around with Lord's traditional opening vamp before the rest of the band get into the act. Gillan fiddles while the others burn, twiddling his phrasing and changing the words on the spot in the style of the blues singers of old.

It's not authentic to the 1972 album version, but it is done in the spirit of experimentation, and the musicianship is first-class. Gillan's two harmonica breaks are spot on, too.

'Keyboard Solo' (Airey, Ammons, Mozart, Rossini)

Here, like on the NEC recording, Airey juggles the blues and classical with great beauty, melding piece upon piece, from 'The William Tell Overture' to the opening section of 'Perfect Strangers'. This is a crazy, magical five minutes that covers so much ground yet feels much shorter.

'Space Truckin''

The symphonic power of the previous track makes this *Machine Head* classic a perfect follow-up. Rarely has the organ and bass united in quite the way they do on this chorus. This seems to inspire Glover even further, and he delivers a nice sliding bass at the very end.

Gillan attempts to give this the vocal power it deserves, but there is a cost: several times, he is unable to do the follow-up line, or he substitutes a lyric with a scream. As good as his screams are, it's obvious they are covering up for his exhaustion.

'Highway Star'

The second of three *Machine Head* tracks to close out the concert, this anthem is identified instantly by the opening snare work. However, Morse snatches it into something different with some soloing, backed closely by Glover, who is still in the improvisation afterglow of the previous track. The music almost imperceptibly increases in power as a bit of instrumental ad-libbing takes place, but not always perfectly, because a couple of times Paice's cues are missed. It all would have been great if it was for a purpose, but it is all a somewhat anaemic introduction. That is until Gillan comes in with his opening scream, forcing everything back in line. Morse's guitar is low in the mix until the ferociously fast solo that challenges the dynamic of the Blackmore recording. Gillan again gravitates between wonderful screams and then being unable to sing all the words, making this a mixed bag vocally. If he was tired after the last number, he is just spent here. And there's still a song to go.

'Smoke On The Water'

As we know, the song has great significance to Montreux and is an apt song to finish the encore, but it has never been introduced like this. Airey turns the riff into a lounge tune. Paice, Morse and Glover join in to deliver something more Dave Brubeck than DP, appropriate perhaps for the Montreux Jazz Festival. It's a lovely bit of lateral thinking that showcases how these players can turn their fingers to any style for the occasion. After two minutes of this, the song proper comes in to the screams of the audience. The verses are dominated, of course, by Gillan's storytelling, but underneath, there is plenty going on with Airey and Morse in sound effects mode to highlight the words. The rhythm develops a tinge of a shuffle, allowing Morse's guitar solo to break some new territory with a jazz edge before the final verse goes back into a straight 4/4, and the song closes out with a series of accents. It is not the most dynamic live version of the song, but few would argue it isn't one of the most interesting.

Now What?! (2013)

Personnel
Ian Gillan: vocals
Steve Morse: guitars
Don Airey: keyboards
Roger Glover: bass
Ian Paice: drums and percussion
Bob Ezrin: backing vocals, percussion
David Hamilton: keyboards
Eric Darken: percussion
Jason Roller: acoustic guitar
Mike Johnson: steel guitar
Record label: earMUSIC
Recorded at The Tracking Room, Rainbow Recorders & Anarchy Studios, Nashville, US, in 2012
Produced by Bob Ezrin
Release date: 26 April 2013
Highest chart places: UK: 19, US: 110
Running time: 57:06

Album Facts

On 16 July 2012, as the band were preparing for the recording of *Now What?!,* Jon Lord died after a year-long battle with cancer. Although he had been out of the band for over a decade, his presence was still felt as they played so many of his co-writes, and there was the familial tie of Paice being married to Lord's wife's twin. It can be no surprise then that Lord's death is felt across the album: two songs mark his passing, and the record itself is dedicated to him.

There was one big change for this album. Former Kiss and Pink Floyd producer Bob Ezrin took over the producing role from Michael Bradford, having approached the band himself after seeing them live. Morse, who had worked with Ezrin in the band Kansas, gave a big vote in favour of the producer.

In a video that came as a bonus with the album, Glover, Paice and Morse agree that Ezrin had a facility for snap decision-making, and this was manifested in the quickness of the recording process, leading to many of the tracks being first takes and some having no overdubs. Indeed, Paice was only in the Nashville studio for ten days, from the initial set-up to the laying down of the last track. Speedy it may have been, but Airey told *The Desert Sun*'s Bruce Fessier in 2015 that Ezrin focussed on the individuals:

> Bob Ezrin said, 'I want to hear you guys playing. That's what I want to record.' And that's what we did. He put us in a really good studio and made sure he had plenty of separation.'

The band also credits Ezrin for encouraging Gillan to move even further away from girls and sex to focus on more stories from everyday life. Gillan had done that before, but his life writing is almost a motif on this album. It would stay a motif for the next decade.

Now What?! shows this maturity through experimentation of styles, a kind of *Purpendicular* for the 2000s. The fans responded to it too, taking it to number one in Germany, Austria and Norway, and although it went no further than 110 on the US *Billboard* chart, it reached a creditable 33 on that country's rock album chart. The band, all now in their 60s, showed an uncharacteristic interest in singles, too, possibly due to Ezrin's influence. The band's new label shared this enthusiasm. DP had been transferred to EDEL's subsidiary earMUSIC, which would have a policy of releasing more than one version of the album, along with live recordings and many singles, digitally and physically. This label's strong promotional focus meant that three of the album's singles reached number three on the UK physical singles chart (the fourth reached number ten), an extraordinary result that proved the new bosses knew their stuff. It seems the band had found a Sympatico label at last.

Album Cover

This is a striking and simple cover. There are none of the artistic pretensions of *Abandon* and *Rapture Of The Deep*. 2013's DP has gone for simplicity, with German artist Antje Warnecke designing a white cover and a bold, clear font for the band and album names. The front is dominated by a huge pairing of question and exclamation marks in the middle. There is a clever tie-in with the question mark replacing the 'P' and the exclamation mark forming the 'L' in Purple. The colour purple is used both in the front and back cover lettering.

The rear of the cover continues the word-based theme with the track names and little else. Although Warnecke's font is a busy mixture of size, case and boldness, it is easy to read. Inside the cover, there is no busyness, just a clear, straight font used for the dedication to Lord.

The band breaks with the recent past by having their photos scattered throughout the booklet. Gillan, with a shorn head, no longer bears any resemblance to the head-banging, long-tressed singer of the 1970s. He, like the rest of the band, is dressed in cool blacks and leg-fitting trousers, an effect enhanced by black & white photography. There is no airbrushing, and it's refreshing.

Warnecke would go on to design the special release versions of the album, the singles' artwork and several covers for live albums, all using the same band name style.

All tracks by Airey, Gillan, Glover, Morse, Paice, Ezrin (unless otherwise noted)

'A Simple Song'

A new producer and a wildly different start to a DP album. What we have is a thoughtful opening bassline, joined in turn by keyboards, guitar (with the space of a Mark Knopfler-style finger-pick), and finally, Gillan, who slides in with a slower vocal cadence. Suddenly, surprisingly, the band comes in with a power worthy of the band's classic openers. Ezrin gives a shining moment to Airey who does one of his most dynamic solos yet. Finally, it all drops away to take us back to Gillan, revisiting his opening lines.

That packs in a lot into a relatively short 4.12. It is a portent that this might be a DP album unlike any other. Given the pall over the album created by Jon Lord's death, there is no surprise that Gillan starts the album by reflecting on ageing, fame and how the joy of being a young rock star inevitably gets lost to the vagaries of life. This is a deep reflection. Has Gillan embraced his age and finally left behind the sex and pub stories? We'll see.

'Weirdistan'

Gillan continues his reflections in a dense, poetic and open-to-interpretation lyric. The track's title is obviously a pointer to something that suggests world affairs, and he mentions borders, flags, stretchers and neighbours, so there is the suggestion of the refugee issue that was so much in the media at the time. All this is a long way from his furious anti-woke messaging of only a couple of albums ago. It's significant also that he doesn't feel the need to scream, emoting instead in his lower register.

The band and producer give him plenty of clear air for these words with a down and grungy backing led by Glover's earthy bass line. Airey's new world synth tones somehow work in unison with the bass, and the ending is also new, with the synth dropping away to let Glover's bass have the last word. All this makes for a great trip of power music.

'Out Of Hand'

It seems like we are going to have the same old keyboard effects intro, but the band quickly sends us in a different direction, giving us instead a synth that has the ominousness of the theme from the Alfred Hitchcock movie *Psycho*.

This time, Gillan tackles human fickleness. It could be about world affairs or his gripes on the music industry. It's a rather depressing message, particularly as he appears to be saying that it is normal human behaviour:

> It's a dirty business it's a crying shame.
> You blink your eye and all the laws have changed.
> They draw you in you hear a siren call.
> Build you up so they can see you fall.
> You've seen it all before.
> Been there since time began.

The music is less interesting than on the first two tracks, although the post-chorus keyboards are pretty snappy. Listen for the moment at the end of the guitar solo as it merges fabulously into a synth run.

'Hell To Pay'

A fast one that is the most like Blackmore's DP, with a punchline that moves into AC/DC or Kiss territory. This track would be proof that Ezrin's speediness mantra was not just lip service. It was recorded so quickly that Airey's organ solo was done live without overdubs.

This is the first story song on the album about a rebellious and somewhat philosophical child (from Gillan's own youth, one can infer) who has a jaundiced view of the world and the future. Gillan slips in his own equally downbeat view of today's education system:

> Annie was a die-hard rebel in the good old days of way back when
> The cigarette was cool and all the kids in school could read and count to ten

There is a fury in the pace, and the guitar and organ solos are competent, as always, but this track breaks little new ground, except for Glover, who has been liberated from tonic notes and is obviously enjoying it. There's a sense that now he's no longer producing, he can concentrate on his own game. Much more than Bradford on the previous two albums, Ezrin is proving good for Glover.

'Bodyline'

Ezrin is a producer who knows that power does not necessarily equate to speed, and Paice's fabulously syncopated intro is an example of that. What also works here is the fact that when the other players enter, they don't swamp. Morse's initial guitar fills the gaps in the drum licks and Glover's bass adds an extra layer. Ditto the synths. It makes for a glorious one-minute groove in the DP catalogue, the sort last seen when Glenn Hughes was funking DP up in the 1970s. There is a bit more busyness ahead with an organ solo that slips into being uncharacteristically intrusive. The drum rhythm remains jaunty and consistent all through, though, so much so that it could go down as Paice's own 'Funky Drummer'.

The lyrics are a return to Gillan's sexy woman stuff. There are signs of something deeper among the sex, including an inexplicable line about fighting for your country. Maybe it's all a metaphor for something grander, but that's doubtful, as elsewhere, the words are on a much more corporeal level. Even rapper Mike Jones gets a mention. Despite its shortcomings, this is a great number that proves what can be done with a little space.

'Above And Beyond'

The first of the two songs on the album dedicated to the memory of Jon Lord is done with a 3/4 time and a riff that Glover once described as 'heavy as fuck'. Indeed it is. Lord was long gone from the band by the time the song was written in the studio, but it channels the strength of his 'Perfect Strangers' work. It is not until more than a minute into the piece that the groove softens for Gillan to pay his tribute:

You draw back your curtain
A wavy goodbye
Lift up your arms
And look up to the sky
To the sky!

Gillan almost talk-sings the verses, but this soon changes into something much more high register as he seems to be speaking for the departed Lord:

I may be leaving
But I won't be gone
I'll be there when you want me
Above and beyond

Then we get to the lines that are the centrepiece of the album:

And tomorrow you'll find
That souls having touched
Are forever entwined

Gillan rarely opens his heart like this in his lyrics.

The final minutes continue the chunky groove but allow the lyrical sentiments to sit with the listener. This goes on right through to the very slow fadeout. No solos, no busy business. This is for Lord, and it could not have been done better. The record-buying public agreed, sending this to the top three in UK vinyl singles sales.

'Blood From A Stone'

A soft opening leads to an almost-spoken verse that contrasts with a short, raucous chorus, which is the protagonist's moment of anger at his situation. And we're talking about a loser here, someone abandoned and who has nothing left to give. Crime is considered and rejected, but the anger remains. Come the song's end, one wishes there was more; that the story is completed. It can't be because this is a mind song; the protagonist is caught in a cycle of circular thinking, pathos, anger and resentment. You get the sense he'd probably still be thinking the same way to this day. Well done, Gillan.

The verses are helped by a piano that gives us a glimpse of a different keyboard style: part-nightclub, part-dreamy. Morse's solo is from the same book, riffing slowly over the Glover-Paice bed. There aren't many reunion DP slow songs that succeed like this one.

'Uncommon Man'

The second track dedicated to Jon Lord, it pays homage to Lord musically as well as in word, and it's done in the most orchestral of ways. Airey takes us back to the progressive Lord style of the Simper/Evans albums of the late 1960s with his fanfare, which develops into a band jam. Fittingly, Airey leads the song into another Lord style, majestic and anthemic. Although it might sound planned and storyboarded, Airey told *The Desert Sun* in 2015 it was a spontaneous reaction to Lord's death:

> We were halfway through recording when the awful news came through that Jon had passed away. We were deeply shocked. So that's a tribute to him. He was an uncommon man.

The lyrics are dramatic, too, speaking of Lord being 20 foot tall and a king.

This is a track that may have been led by Airey, but Morse entwines his solos with him, merging beautifully into the keyboard fanfare again and again.

A masterful track in the grandest of ways and another fitting tribute.

'Aprés Vous'

This is rollicking, thick, heavy, and even ferocious, and on fan forums, it is cited as being among the favourites. In his *Drumtribe* podcast in 2022, Paice reveals that this track was done in the old style, in one take with no stitching together of elements, although a click track was used.

The lyrics are fascinating. Aprés Vous means 'after you', which fits since the lyric seems to be a rear-vision examination of the fleetingness of fame:

> We went from chosen few and our confidence grew
> Depends on where you're standing
> Despite what you think
> It's only a blink between take-off and landing

The words may be a new take on the swiftness of life, but not everything about the song feels original. The bridges are like those on 'Back To Back' and there are, inexplicably, echoes of 'Bodyline' from the same album. Some of the rhyming couplets were starting to sound like what we had heard before. After all the progressive work and Lord tributes, it sounds a little like the band was starting to run out of ideas. Ezrin did like to get songs down in only a couple of takes, but sometimes music needs a closer listen to check it hasn't fallen into existing tropes. It happened here and didn't need to.

'All The Time In The World'

Gillan returns to the time theme on which he started the album. When earlier, he said time didn't matter; here, he says there's plenty of it, so there's no need to hurry. Gillan's eclecticism is also on show here, with references to Achilles and the ancient Greek philosopher Zeno of Elea. One can't help but think this also relates to the death of his old friend Lord since he once again references the band's early days.

Musically, Gillan is happy to let his bandmates take the lead. In a couple of places early on, each chorus is swamped so badly by keyboards that Gillan can barely be heard. Morse, however, is restraint itself, giving us one of his few half-time solos.

The ending is something new. Bass drum and bass do beats that fade, like a dying heartbeat. It suits the sentiments of the song and the album perfectly.

'Vincent Price'

Perhaps they thought that after all this self-reflective stuff, they needed to end the album with something completely different. After all, no one, apart from maybe Nick Cave, wants to have their albums remembered as the ones about life and death. And death especially.

Still, it's a funny choice this one: a paean to Vincent Price, who was a major B-horror film star when Gillan was a lad. It's ironic that on this album dedicated to a lost chum, Price's movies were invariably about grisly murders and the afterlife.

There could be a simpler explanation. Given that the album was recorded out of a series of jams and half-thoughts, it's entirely possible that the horror organ notes that open the song were Airey improvisations that everyone jumped on. Certainly, the very simple lyrics sound thrown together:

> Deep in the dungeon
> There's a rattling of chains
> Mad Dr Phibes
> Gonna eat my brains

Morse and Airey throw in some horror movie twangs and the singing has an off-kilter tone. It would be interesting to know exactly what is being sung under the two bridges; the singer is mixed so low that his words give no more than just the effect of a horror chorus. At the end of the song (and thus the album), Gillan gives his highest scream for quite some time. It's a lovely note to finish on and, given the tone of the song, just perfect. It was the second single from the album, and just like 'Above And Beyond' and 'All The Time In The World', it also reached number three in physical sales in the UK. This makes this album the most successful singles charter for a long time.

'It'll Be Me' (Jack Clement) (Deluxe Edition bonus)
The bonus track is a straight cover, the first the reunion band had committed to a studio album since 'Hush'. Jerry Lee Lewis did the original, and it has been covered by many people, including Cliff Richard.

DP's mid-tempo version is a simple take, probably coming out of a jam that was put to one side during the sessions. It is competent but nothing particularly new.

'First Sign Of Madness' (B-side of Vincent Price & a gold edition bonus)
A great groove track that would have been an interesting diversion on the album proper. Busy as busy can be and really tight, it has as highlights a honky piano solo, Morse's very fast fingerwork, and great fast rhythm section work, led by Glover's bass, which holds it together. Airey, Gillan and Morse dance on top, giving real meaning to the term 'bonus track'.

InFinite (2017)

Personnel
Ian Gillan: vocals
Steve Morse: guitars
Don Airey: keyboards
Roger Glover: bass
Ian Paice: drums and percussion
Bob Ezrin: backing vocals, keyboards, percussion
Tommy Denander: guitar
Record label: earMUSIC
Recorded at The Tracking Room & Anarchy Studios, Nashville, US, in February 2017
Produced by Bob Ezrin
Release date: 7 April 2017
Highest chart places: UK: 6, US: 105
Running time: 45:37

Album Facts

InFinite may be the most ironic album title in the DP catalogue. Birthed on the cusp of the *Long Goodbye Tour*, the band could obviously see an end to all this touring business. Gillan told *Classic Rock*'s Paul Rees at the time that age was certainly part of the album naming decision:

> We're all knocking on a bit. I walk down the road and hear a clang on the pavement – something else has dropped off.

Hardly rock star stuff. And in June, it seemed it could be all over because, in Stockholm, Paice suffered a mini-stroke, waking with the right side of his body numb and with no control over his right hand and fingers. Gillan told *Classic Rock*'s Stef Lach a year later that other band members had also been unwell, and so it could've ended there:

> It was suggested that we call it a day. We supposed it had to end sooner or later. But we're all feeling better now.

Despite the health issues, the band ended the year with some cheer. It was announced that they would be inducted into the Rock & Roll Hall Of Fame, but even this did not come without its controversies. The band's first singer, Rod Evans, was included, but the bassist of that time, Nick Simper, was not. Neither were current members Steve Morse and Don Airey, *Come Taste The Band* guitarist Tommy Bolin, nor *Slaves & Masters* singer Joe Lynn Turner. Ritchie Blackmore was included, but he didn't turn up to the ceremony (there had been a minor contretemps about playing on the night, with Gillan refusing to have Blackmore replacing Morse for the gig. Whether this was the real reason for the no-show, only Blackmore knows).

On the back of this Hall Of Fame impetus, the band returned to the studio for the first time in five years to record what would become *InFinite*. The tracks were laid down at Ezrin's usual rapidity at the same two Nashville studios that had been used for *Now What?!* The group's bonhomie and rapid progress were also recorded in a documentary by Sky Arts TV, which was released as the cleverly titled *From Here To InFinity*.

In August 2018, Glover told *Bass Guitar Magazine*'s Andy Hughes that Ezrin made his presence felt strongly on the album, going as far as to insist on what instruments should be played:

> He brought in a Precision (bass guitar), and from its look, the strings were put on back in the 1800s! I said we'd have to change the strings. No, Bob said very clearly. It'd been played on Pink Floyd albums and albums by Peter Gabriel and Alice Cooper, so we can't change the strings. Lots of people have played this bass because it sounds really well. He was right. It did sound really good.

At just under 46 minutes, *InFinite* is the shortest studio album since *Perfect Strangers*, but this didn't stop it from continuing the band's slow move up the charts. It reached number six in the UK (the highest of any reunion album, just edging out *Perfect Strangers*) and 16 on the US Top Rock Albums. It didn't quite crack the broader *Billboard* 100 but came very close. It also hit the top in Germany and Switzerland and had a single hit number one in physical sales in the UK. The Ezrin experiment was proving its worth.

The Long Goodbye Tour took place soon after the release, and part of it was a co-headlining tour with Judas Priest. In 2017, Gillan told *Uncut*'s John Robinson that, as the name suggested, it was probably their last time on the road. He spoke too soon.

Album Cover

After the simplicity of the previous album, the band returns to a graphic-based design, but on a grand scale. Snow and cold are the themes this time. The front cover is an image of an icebreaker going through a frozen sea. It has left a dark trail, which is in the form of the latest DP logo, which combines the cursive D and P into a form that is the mathematical sign for infinity. The band name and the album title are across the top and are in yet another new font. It was designed by German graphic designer Dirk Rudolph. Rudolph also produced bespoke covers for this album's singles and the *From Here To Infinite* DVD.

On the back cover, the band are heavily dressed in snow attire, including goggles, with the icebreaker ship looming heavily in the background. There is also a nice touch of a flag with the new DP logo on it. The only script is the list of the band members in the top centre. Interestingly, egalitarianism seems to have gone out the window. The three Mk 2 members are listed alphabetically. Then comes Morse, with Airey last.

It is refreshing that, once again, the band are not trying to look like groovy young rockers. The light is unflattering, and they look like they don't care a fig about hiding wrinkles.

Snow was also used extensively in the special edition booklets and publicity, with images showing the band standing alongside snow dogs, sledges and skis. There is a contrasting image of the band resting in a warm room with a couple of the dogs, drinking something probably very alcoholic. The map on the wall tells us that the band are supposed to be in Antarctica.

All tracks by Airey, Gillan, Glover, Morse, Paice, Ezrin (unless otherwise noted)

'Time For Bedlam'

It's a reasonable assumption that the title, 'Time For Bedlam' would point to this track being no-holds-barred. But it was not quite that kind of song. The opening is certainly daring, with a set of synth strings that could have come from a scene in a slasher movie. The singing is equally interesting, being heavily SFX'd into an atonal chant like that of an orthodox priest. Gillan told Umberto Sulpasso that he and Glover thought up the song's title as a humorous thing, but rather than going for heavy thrash, they decided it should be more of a social commentary piece:

> So, we just write an impressionist version of... some frustrations about institutions and that sort of thing that we'd love to escape from.

This protest story centres on Bedlam, London's 770-year-old insane asylum. Gillan banishes a political prisoner to the asylum, but then a change into mid-tempo rock moves the lyrical perspective from the narrator to the victim, who describes how he managed to survive. Gillan's previous lyrics have been critical of political correctness, of the music industry, of wowsers, and the words could apply cleanly to any of these:

> No pity, no pity
> Don't want no pity for me in this filthy cell
> I'll see you in hell
> See you in hell

Airey and Morse answer Gillan, adding to the slightly off-kilter vibe. They are light, almost carnival, and this isn't a light and carnival song. Obviously, the intention is to create a musical madness. The problem is that they sound like they're trying to create a musical madness. It might seem odd then that this is the first single from the album, but it was obviously a wise decision since it hit number one on the physical single chart in the UK in February 2017, making it a high for the reunion band.

'Hip Boots'

After the ambitious historical otherworldliness of the opening track, we come back to earth with this blues number about how much Gillan loves his shoes. Well, he could be talking about personas rather than clothing apparel, but the point is moot. The track takes us nowhere new or exciting. Like on the opening track, the highlight is the chorus and Gillan's chants. But that's not enough to carry a song. It does start to feel that the organ and guitar solos are something we have experienced before, even if they are delivered with an intensity worthy of the DP name. There are a couple of verses and those well-executed choruses and then it's over. This is one of the few DP album tracks that, in word and music, fails to connect on an emotional level despite Gillan's claim to Umberto Sulpasso that it has its origins in chain gang blues music.

'All I Got Is You'

This sounds more like it. You might expect the fine snare drum work from Paice to be joined by huge roaring guitars, but the tale takes another turn with Airey-on-Airey synth work.

Gillan's lyrics are a development on the argument-with-the-missus theme already explored in 'Girls Like That', 'Clearly Quite Absurd' and 'I Got Your Number'. Here, though, he's fighting back, and it's not always subtle:

> You make stupid accusations
> By which time I've lost the thread
> Sometimes I wonder how it is you get
> To piss me off this much

There is no reconciliation, no admission of wrongdoing. It just goes on to an ultimately cruel ending:

> To be honest with you, babe
> I'm only in it for the ride
> You may never bring yourself
> To take me as I am
> But in case you haven't noticed
> I don't give a fucking damn

The music is finely done. Morse and Airey trill beautifully in sync, and the band does a lovely ascension halfway through. The ending is equally strong, matching Gillan's final kiss-off. It is a well-executed power song dragged down by an unappetising and, at times, pedestrian lyric.

Given that it is hardly uplifting stuff, it is odd that Gillan would refer to it as a fun little thing that developed off a line that Paice dropped once in the studio: 'You've got me, but all I've got is you.' It was probably also an odd song to be promoted as a centrepiece of the album, but it was released as the second single and got the full marketing treatment. This includes a music video that begins in the streets of Nashville as the band are recording. Interestingly, the band look bemused as Gillan sings, as if wondering what this is all about. In the video, Gillan is reading his words and jiggles his shoulders to the music, but he doesn't seem particularly committed to either. Hearing the audio alone, though, he sounds more than a trifle angry.

The music video is very tell-me, show-me, with his words about drinking overlaid with Glover drinking. The line about packing a suitcase shows Morse putting his guitar in a bag. It is way too literal, very silly, and had no effect on helping the song to chart, which it didn't.

'One Night In Vegas'

Gillan's story songs have extended from the surprisingly successful ('Smoke On The Water') to the oddball ('Mitzi Dupree'). Sometimes, he is so inspired by a true event that he combines truth with his most masterful writing, such as in 'Somebody Stole My Guitar'. It's a risk, depending on what story Gillan uses as his inspiration.

'One Night in Vegas' tells the story of a man who is dead drunk in Las Vegas, and in a twist at the end, his life changes. Gillan sings the story with conviction as if it had really happened. It did. Gillan had heard about a man who married a woman he just met on a drunken night in Las Vegas. The kicker for Gillan was that 30 years later, they were still together.

The band offers another strong backing, dominated by Airey's double-time piano part that fits right in, possibly because of the Vegas nightclub imagery that is carried across the song. The music creates a semi-chaotic vibe that matches the character's confusion and excess.

This proves that Ezrin's advice about storytelling could lead to the goods being produced.

'Get Me Outta Here'

An atypically heavy drum groove recorded using what sounds to be a kit microphone opens proceedings in a mode like Led Zeppelin's 'When The Levee Breaks', except Paice funks it up with fast snare work.

The story itself is another of Gillan's slice-of-life sagas. This time, he is an unemployed father who is living rough and harks back to more carefree days. In the end, there is no revelation or desire to change. He just wants to flee. Coupled with some earlier songs on the album, Gillan could appear to be building a set of sociological stories. He isn't, of course. These stories of his have no beginning, middle and end. He just gives us a character thinking in a moment, as he has done on some earlier work. The track is dark and both guitar and keyboard solos reek of the central character's desperation. But it is Paice's echoed drums that mark it out in stone.

At 3.59, it is the third shortest track on the album and never outstays its welcome, even if the sudden ending has a feel of unfinished business.

'The Surprising'

As surprising as the title suggests, this track is the closest producer Ezrin comes to dragging the band into the kind of territory he took Kiss on *Destroyer.* That album was an extraordinary blend of the gothic, the anthemic and the sex-focused. Here, after tracks about low-lives and misogynists, we have a joined suite of styles that, for the most part, work together to take the listener on a trip that promises to be ethereal right from Airey's horror movie opening. Gillan called it a story about temptation set in surreal terms. Gillan's lyrics, which reference an Egyptian king and a biblical figure, are backed by a slew of experiments by the rest of the band. Daringly, the music then morphs towards a quasi-country territory. Finally, Nashville switches into progressive at 2.02 when Airey gives us a line that could have come directly from DP's earliest canon. It is toughened up by some clever snare from Paice (whose work is quickly becoming the highlight of this album).

If Lord had been involved in this song, it would have set out as a movement proper. Here, the band has done something different but just as extraordinary: they put together a suite that is as stunning as anything from the early days without charts or planned layouts. Many DP albums have centrepieces. This is one of them. It's not perfect but damned close.

'Johnny's Band'

This starts as if it is following on from the progressiveness of 'The Surprising'. However, as has been the case so many times before, things change into a kind of 4/4 straightness.

Gillan gives us another story, a semi-autobiographical one about a musician who got a band together. The band was successful, played lots of gigs, wowed audiences and had hit records. Then drugs intervened and they split up and lost money before finally playing small venues, apparently happy again.

And that's it. It could be the story of most bands, even DP itself, but they are not terribly involving lyrics, having none of the emotion, for example, of Dire Straits' similarly themed 'Sultans Of Swing'.

Sadly, this, one of the weakest tracks on the album, was chosen as the third and final single from the album. Once again, no cigar.

'On Top Of The World'

The story here tells of a true incident at a party with Kuala Lumpur sex workers after a Gillan gig in the early 1980s. The basics are that the girls took Gillan onto a roof, frolics were had and everyone passed out. The next morning, the singer woke with a mouth full of rice. The perfect woman he had spent time with the night before was less so in the morning light. This was a self-deprecating true yarn with an ending that suggested he fell from the 20th floor. Dramatic licence, obviously.

The music, with its dirty grunge, fits this slight story perfectly. The music suddenly ends, and Gillan takes up the story as if he is a god delivering a passage from the bible. Given the story matter, this is a strange choice, particularly when he starts talking about cockroaches. But there is a good punchline and the music returns in all its glorious lethargy, bang on cue.

This song is another case of a lot of style being put into little substance, but it's a fun journey.

'Birds Of Prey'

Obviously, someone had been listening to Led Zeppelin. For the second time on the album, Paice's drums have that heavy John Bonham echo. But where Led Zep gave their drummer all the space in the world to his canon/drums, here Paice is closely marked by Morse's riffing. It's a very good opening gambit, nonetheless.

The words are worth the wait. Gillan moves away from his story-type lyrics to political commentary:

> Bad news travels at the speed of flight
> Good news not at all
> And here we are again

Gillan told Sulpasso that the song is about aggression, particularly religious aggression. The title comes from how warmongers are like birds of prey who rip things to pieces without qualification.

What is new about this lyric is that the words are scattered in snatches throughout, broken up by blocks of musical ingenuity from the guitar and keyboards. There is no straitjacket of a verse/chorus/verse/middle eight structure.

The track, with its gravitas and simple protestations, could be something from the Moody Blues' masterpiece *A Question Of Balance*.

After a collection of songs that have ranged from superb to downright strange, this would have been a magnificent moment to end the album, particularly if it was to be DP's final work.

Except someone must have suggested they needed to finish on an upbeat note.

'Roadhouse Blues' (Jim Morrison)

Although there were some unused tracks left in the can, it was decided that this classic from The Doors was just the thing to puncture the seriousness of 'Birds Of Prey'.

As with 'It'll Be Me' and 'Bludsucker' before it, this version proves the adage that a cover must offer something new to be worth the bother. It starts very well, with Paice offering a great groove that gives no clue about the song that's about to hit.

When it is revealed, we hear Gillan scat a little, play some saucy harmonica, and be joined by some Airey honky-tonk, backed by a nice walking bass. Airey ramps up his beerhouse piano into a killer solo. In DP's hands, 'Roadhouse Blues' has become a blues song in every sense.

Vocally, though, Gillan rarely gets out of second gear. A few Gillan highs would have been magic over the top of this background. Instead, he lets his harmonica do the speaking and it speaks well, leaving us with a deep blues born out of collective memory and five lifetimes of experience.

Yes, this one was worth the bother.

'Paradise Bar' (Limited Edition bonus)

Just why this one was left to be a bonus track is anyone's guess. It is a heartfelt piece that merges into something very like 'Uncommon Man' from *Now What?!* Gillan says the lyric is about a man who dies in a car accident and meets himself and others in a bar in heaven. Perhaps someone noticed the similarity in the fanfare to 'Uncommon Man', the instrumental version of which was already in the works as a bonus track. Despite its similarities to several other songs in the canon, it has a verve of its own, led all the way by Airey's keyboards. It would have been a better choice for the album than, say, 'Johnny's Band'.

'Simple Folk' (Morse) (Limited Edition bonus)

Just as 'Paradise Bar' was Airey's song, this short stab of gentle playing is all Morse. Unaccompanied and roughly recorded, it is loaded with emotional connection. If just for the contrast, DP could have done with more of this kind of stuff.

'Uncommon Man' (Limited Edition bonus instrumental)

The Jon Lord tribute from the previous album, minus the voice. As an instrumental, it takes on a new life without the distraction of a vocal over the top, as good as the vocal was. It's just that the music on its own was spectacular in a way that Lord, the concerto composer, would have appreciated. It was a fine decision to add this as an extra, although one may question why it wasn't done on the previous album as a bonus alongside the worded version.

'Above And Beyond' (Limited Edition bonus instrumental)

As with 'Uncommon Man', this *Now What?!* track is stunning. It is less successful as a voiceless version, however, because Gillan's voice was so central to the earlier production, his melody leading into each section is more effective than any Paice fill. Without the voice, it sometimes sounds just like a backing track. It's still an interesting listen, though.

'Hip Boots Rehearsal' (Limited Edition bonus)
One might think this is scraping the bottom of the vault's floor (being Ian Paice's own recording of the instrumental backing), but it was worth the inclusion if only to show what this song is like without Gillan's voice. It sounds like an entirely different track. And for a personal recording, it comes up nicely.

'Strange Kind Of Woman' (Live in Aalborg bonus)
This track is not mixed particularly well, with guitar wails and keyboards blasting out over the cardboard-sounding drums. We've heard it all before live, and better. This feels like the result of someone's desperation for bonus material.

Whoosh! (2020)

Personnel
Ian Gillan: vocals
Steve Morse: guitars
Don Airey: keyboards
Roger Glover: bass
Ian Paice: drums and percussion
Ayana George: backing vocals
Tiffany Palmer: backing vocals
Record label: earMUSIC
Recorded at The Tracking Room, Anarchy & Ocean Way, Nashville, US; Henson, Los Angeles, US; Noble Street, Toronto, Canada, between 2019 and 2020
Produced by Bob Ezrin
Release date: 7 August 2020
Highest chart places: UK: 4, US: 161
Running time: 51:29 (including the bonus track)

Album Facts

Bob Ezrin returns to produce his third DP album, and again he records in Nashville, and again swiftly. Given this, it may seem odd that this feels like a very slowly manicured offering, with delicately overlaid and spaced instruments and lyrics crafted with great thoughtfulness.

It may not have happened at all, though, because after *InFinite* was released, Morse suggested that the band finish up, saying it would be ending on a high. It was a suggestion that didn't go down well with the others. Given this reluctance to end the band, there is a surprising finality theme throughout, with life-questioning tropes. Even the album title speaks of endings. Glover said (in a conversation video with Bob Ezrin in 2019) that it came from a *Fawlty Towers* TV show episode:

> When John Cleese is at some point doing his rant in the kitchen, he goes 'whoosh' and 'What's that?' and 'That's your life mate.'

This album may have been the result of *InFinite*'s chart success (105 in the US), but it was to reach only 161 in that country, a considerable fall. It was a different story in the UK, where it reached number four, the highest position for any post-reunion studio album (in fact, the highest since 1973's *Burn*). Like *Now What?!* and *InFinite,* it got the top spot in the UK's 'Rock & Metal' chart, although it was far from a metal album. It also topped the charts in several other countries, justifying the choice to make this lineup's most inventive and, at times, most progressive album. The typically understated Paice said the songs on the album worked well together, and many critics agreed. *NME*'s Leonie Cooper called it: 'the most stupidly fun and outrageously silly album of the year.' *Classic Rock*'s Paul Brannigan labelled it 'playful and powerful'.

It is all those things.

Album Cover

The cover, designed by Milan-based graphic designers Jekyll & Hyde (with a credit for additional artwork to Jenny Seiler), has the dynamic imagery of a dissolving astronaut, which had been used for the final shot in the music video for the single, 'Throw My Bones'. The concept came from band management, who offered several image ideas, and the band went for the astronaut. Gillan told Greg Prato that this image of decay can be taken in several ways:

> I think some of the guys looked at the lyrics and saw the apocalyptic nature of some of these scenarios and came up with the dissolving spaceman, which I kind of like. And in a more humorous sense, it describes Deep Purple's career. Like, Whoosh! – it seems like just yesterday it was 1970. It seemed to fit.

The apocalypse Gillan talks about is heightened by the Mars-like sand that has a red reflection. A detail in the image is the framing marks up each side and across the bottom as if the view of the dissolving man is coming from a video monitor or another astronaut. Across the top is the band name, and once again, the font for the band name seems new, although it is very close to the one used on their first album, *Shades Of Deep Purple* (and on Paice's bass drumhead on the subsequent tours). It's another clue that the band was thinking of finishing where it had begun. The booklet and gatefold artwork take highlights from the sand tones. In the middle, the disintegration theme is carried to the maximum: instead of the astronaut turning to dust, it is the earth that is disintegrating. Message received.

All tracks by Airey, Gillan, Glover, Morse, Paice, Ezrin (unless otherwise noted)

'Throw My Bones'

No synths and no slow opening. This album begins just like *Purpendicular* and *Abandon* with a solid groove that says this is all about rock with a touch of funk thrown in. Gillan's lyric also gets straight to it with his pondering of what lies ahead. Ezrin says the song was chosen as the opener because it sets the tone for the album, although it was written for *InFinite* and not finished properly until this time around.

This is a brave place to start the album, seemingly confirming that this was going to be DP's last original work. Gillan is in grateful mode. He knows what he has and professes that he has all he needs, so why keep running around? Like John Lennon's 'Watching The Wheels' 40 years before, Gillan is watching and reflecting, but from the perspective of a 75-year-old man who was nearly twice the age Lennon was when he expressed the same thoughts.

As for the cryptic title, in 2020, Gillan told Greg Prato that it had to do with the unknown:

> Throw My Bones is something that people did in prehistoric times to see if it was going to rain tomorrow or if they were going to be alive tomorrow.

Airey's wall-of-sound keyboard is subservient to the vocal, and a very good vocal it is, too, with Gillan moving up the octave easily. The guitar solo flits between pickups, pick position and pedal sounds. Everyone resists the urge to embellish and just let the song fade out simply, allowing its sentiments to have their resonance.

The song was the first single off the album and its video is equally ethereal, starting with a view of Earth from space. An astronaut lands on Earth (oddly, with the cover artwork from the previous album, *InFinite,* reflecting off the visor of the helmet). The spaceman walks alongside traffic, pedestrians, sports players and even a dog who strangely doesn't seem to notice him. Finally, our man sheds some of his space suit until, at the very end, he disintegrates to match the image on the album cover. The band's videos over the years have been a hit-and-miss story, but here, it captures the feel of the song so right. It reached number 11 on the UK Physical Singles chart but deserved to do better.

'Drop The Weapon'

We begin with an interesting, almost Who-like intro that is too quickly swamped by drums and vocals, but very smart vocals they are. They are an advice column for someone who is thinking about going violent. The target could range from some kid in a gang, a partner in a quarrelsome relationship, the Black Lives Matter violence of the time, or just the head of a nation. What's interesting is that it doesn't matter. Gillan's message applies to any of these and other scenarios. At times, the lyrics are basic: 'drop the weapon', to the sublime:

> Come and hold my hand
> Then we can all stand
> And say a prayer
> To someone out there
> Anyone out there

Paice's drums are up front, and that's a good thing because the urgency of the song calls for it: his snare hits are propelling and his fills have an almost military feeling. Glover's bass is solid, playing between the snare hits with great beauty, so it is strange that he has complained that this track's riff, written by Morse, is the most difficult he has ever played. There are the solos, of course, but in this context, they are there to give a sense of disorder by being busy rather than brilliant.

'We're All The Same In The Dark'

This song was recorded once as a live take. A nicely syncopated opening blends well into the vocals, Gillan sliding in over the top with a style that is quite unusual for him: gentle, urging, supplicating, almost. The story starts like a plea between lovers until the clues fall in. Mexico is mentioned (and this was the period when Donald Trump was building walls) and then come the telling lines:

There's no difference 'tween me and you
To tell the truth now
We're all the same in the dark

That would seem to seal it. It seems to be a reminder that no good can come out of us-versus-them thinking. After the preceding song, which was a call for peace, this is a subtle extension of the sentiment.

The music is slinky and bluesy, again with the drums high in the mix, relegating Morse's solo lower than the background keyboards when it should have been the centrepiece. Ezrin would say that the backing vocals, which provide a kind of wall of sound, were one of his favourite parts of the piece.

It's a short song, one of six, that clocks in at around 3.30. The sentiment was expressed, so producer Ezrin saw no great value in outstaying the welcome. The groove on this is so cool that more just might have been better.

'Nothing At All'

DP is not really a compound time band. It is a syncopating, bluesy rock, occasionally funky band, but triple time within a 4/4 beat has not been its agenda. Until this album. And don't Airey and Morse love it with their question-and-answer fanfare breaks. Airey almost takes it into the realm of the fairground but is held to this side of it by Morse's guitar interjections.

It is hard to imagine Blackmore ever allowing this kind of music on one of his DP albums. It is less a redefinition of DP music than a side excursion.

Gillan, once again, is talking about the bigger picture:

Just a few of us walk arm in arm
It's innocent and charming
But the children seem to be getting alarmed
Don't worry kids, it's nothing at all

But a couple of verses in, the true message comes out:

And the junk that sails our seven seas
Is very nearly up to my knees
But the platitudes and pleasantries
Keep saying it's nothing at all

It's not nothing at all, then. There is plenty to be concerned about, particularly Mother Nature, who will have her revenge over the 'it's nothing at all' attitude that is at the root of environmental damage. Gillan's words here are profound yet subtle in tone. That is a feat, considering the deliberately off-kilter vibe that pervades the song. All this makes the track the emotional crux of the album.

Perhaps for this reason, this was chosen as the album's third single. The decidedly odd music video shows a young gent in a bowler hat walking the English countryside and coming across an alien egg and the spaceman from the album cover. The man is seen dragging a net that quickly fills with sea rubbish. The video is visually compelling but so confusing that you can see why it did nothing to improve sales. This is a shame because this enthralling, swirling song demands repeated attention. It adds up to much more than its parts.

'No Need To Shout'

So, after three songs that chew our ears about what's wrong with the world, we have a song that criticises, in the strongest lyrical terms, people who preach. Maybe Gillan is being ironic here, but I don't think so. He's too angry to be playing subtleties.

> You preach to the converted, it's insane
> We're here already swinging like a train
> I can only hope, that you won't
> Ram it down my throat

The first draft of the chorus apparently had the line 'Shut your mouth and fuck off,' but because it didn't rhyme, it was changed to 'Shut your mouth and go away.' Less powerful, perhaps, but it did rhyme.

The music is a step into the past, with an opening organ chord that echoes that of 'Perfect Strangers'. After this, it's pure hard rock. It propels, as Ezrin noted, like a train. The solos bear little relevance to the words, being bright and lively when the lyrics are dour.

Like a few of the earlier tracks, this one is over quickly. Given how the album is progressing, it is around this point that we can see why they divided the album into two acts. A story might be being told here, song by song. By the way, Paice lists this as one of his five favourite DP songs.

'Step By Step'

If there was a story building on the album, this one could be the next step or a huge step away. Gillan sings about someone intruding into his life, a politician perhaps, or the thought police. Or he could be giving us one of his get-out-of-my-life anti-love songs. Whichever it is, his lyrics are getting darker by the song.

The music is a fabulous contrast, being a slow, almost waltz-like, 6/8 time signature, with a chord sequence that Glover would describe as Procol Harum-esque. The influence of the classically trained Airey relishes the chance to get away from the 4/4 timing, which has dominated so much of the last four albums. He throws in keyboard flourishes using a pipe organ sample, with Glover riding him across the song. The middle eight (which is literally in the middle of the song) attempts to be an antidote to the song's off-kilter timing by, intriguingly, being even more off-kilter. This is heightened when Ezrin swirls the drums at the highest points.

The band are trying new things on this album. Instead of having many styles within the one song, here they are mostly one style, one song and then move on. This works in the grandest of ways.

'What The What'

This is the first song on the second side of the record (being the seventh track highlights how short the tracks have been), and it takes us away from the worries of the world into the personal worries of a gallivanting lead singer. We get a tour through bars where there's dancing, sex among unlikelys, too much money spent and a few fights. This is the spiritual sequel of 'Razzle Dazzle' from *Bananas*. There's nothing especially deep except perhaps a celebration of life, which does, in a way, fit into the tone of this album.

The music is also a lot like 'Razzle Dazzle' in that it has a 1950s rock n' roll vamp style, including the occasional piano glissando. Morse's guitar solo fits in with this Chuck Berry feel before delving into something much more contemporary. There are some other effective moments, such as the cool hook refrain of 'so bad'. Now, there's nothing wrong with going backwards in time, but in the framework of an album that has been stretching band boundaries, this does feel like a bonus track at best, although the band nails the style.

'The Long Way Round'

This track takes us into hard rock, a genre that has been mostly absent to this point.

The words are cryptic and may well not make any sense at all:

You can't get me down
I got the 'Things are looking up' blues
I know it happens
But it never sticks to my shoes

As the words go on, Gillan talks about being taken by surprise by someone somewhere. If he means his sacking from the band, then that would be revisiting ancient history. If he is talking about time, then it would be apt for a man who might be thinking he was recording his last original work:

It's been a long time coming
I never thought it would last
I think about the future
Who knows what might have happened in the past?

By this time, Gillan had been regularly into meditation, eating a better diet, and caring for his body. It all shows up well on this song. He is clear. He is sharp.

The first half of the song is dominated by a guitar and synth pairing, but the spark is a little less bright than earlier on the album – but then it shifts into something new with a chorus wall of voices. The guitar and voice answer each other for a short section before we go back to the 1960s with a galloping snare and bass interplaying with organ signatures. A lot of work went into the final section, with some charming keyboard work capped off by a spacey, time-is-slowing finale.

This may not be the greatest song in the catalogue, but it builds to something in the last part that could be considered classic DP.

'The Power Of The Moon'

The world messaging of the first side is back here; this time, it's about the power of nature. Gillan begins his song journey by asking some universal questions:

Who am I to say things may not all be what they seem?
And how can I disturb the facts of life?
And who am I to speak about the fabric of a dream?
And who's to say that dreams cannot be right?

He then attempts to answer them in four stanzas and a two-line chorus before finally concluding that the world keeps turning and will continue to do so. He could also be interpreted as talking about his own mind and how his thinking in the past may have been wrong.

It's a surprisingly introspective song whose sentiments could be easily missed in the thrum of the music accompanying it. It is also apt for the theme of the lyrics: gentle, ethereal, with a lovely turn of overdubbed voice in the chorus.

Not that it's simple. The vocal melody sits almost in opposition to the music, with shifting harmonies underneath. Glover would call the structure weird, and it is weird and not at all ill at ease with itself. Morse and Airey deliver perhaps too literal 1950s sci-fi tones (they obviously heard the 'moon' in the lyrics and went for it). The ending has a coolness, with a pointed piano part that might have come straight out of the Tubes' *The Completion Backwards Principle* and a funky bassline in the passenger seat for the long fadeout.

'Remission Possible'

This tiny snippet at 1.38 is the second shortest track in the DP catalogue. It is really a leader piece for 'Man Alive', which was earmarked as a single (and so probably would not have been radio-friendly with this intro attached). As a result, this is extremely slight but is nicely led by a strong bassline. The frantic rhythm stops at 1.02 to allow Airey to synth it out for the last 40 seconds, leading into the next track.

'Man Alive'

This is the second single from the album and close to its longest track (just beaten by the not-quite-as-good 'The Long Way Round'). Although the producer saw fit to put 'And The Address' on the album as the closer, this track would have been the perfect tie-up, explaining the whole astronaut/environment/extinction theme that pervaded the album artwork.

Gillan delivers another quasi-religious chant before we have a straight rock beat. Gillan's sardonic spoken sections talk about an imaginary future where humanity wipes itself out:

After some thousands of years
Fewer than the smallest imaginable intake of breath
The wisest guys in the evolution of humanity became extinct

Any assumption that this is a COVID song would be wrong. The song was recorded before the virus went pandemic. It's about environment, war and bad human behaviour on a global scale. The band has touched on this theme before, but briefly, way back in 1984 on the reunion album, with the video for 'Knocking At Your Back Door' being equally *Mad Max* in its extinction scenario. So, we are in a full circle. In the 1984 song, the words had absolutely nothing to do with the sentiments of the video. In this case, the video relates perfectly to the lyrics and with no subtlety at all. The astronaut wanders through a series of environments, changing colours as he walks. Forests become deserts and nuclear power stations; ice spaces become industrial sites; lakes become dry beds; beautiful vistas become cities. There are shots of rubbish piles and polluting smokestacks. All this is interspersed with space nebulas and black holes. Then we get the final message:

And something washed up on the beach
A man alive
A man alone
Washed up on the beach
Just a man
Whoosh

Then, we have a live string section playing over the top of an emerging ticking clock.

Needless to say, there was never anything like this in the Blackmore days.

'And The Address Blackmore' (Lord)

This is the third time DP has cannibalised their back catalogue for a post-reunion album, after 'Hush' and 'Bludsucker'. This one, though, is far more interesting because the original song came from an album that not only pre-dated the Gillan/Glover era but was written by Jon Lord and Ritchie Blackmore, both of whom were no longer in the band. More importantly, this track was the first song on the very first DP album. Coming as it does at the very end of *Whoosh!,* is the band trying to tell us something about ending where they started? It was a spritely song in 1968 and a worthy album opener then. It has not significantly changed from the original, except for the dropping of the strange (and very long) progressive opening and the addition of new guitar and organ solos and some drum fills. The mix is so much better balanced here, revealing just how good the writing was all those years ago. There might be an argument for revisiting more of the oldies down the track.

'Dancing In My Sleep' (bonus)

Now that the album proper is over, this track was appended at the end. And this is the proper place for it. It's a light, playful number with an interesting tone, set by the effects at the start that tie in with the spaceman cover concept. The words, though, have nothing remotely other-worldly about them. This is purely love and lust stuff. After the musical brilliance of 'And The Address', which was a great album closer, this should be seen for what it is, a bonus bit of business stuck on the end of the album a-la 'Her Majesty' on The Beatles *Abbey Road*. This is a well-executed bit of business, but not much more than that.

Turning To Crime (2021)

Personnel
Ian Gillan: vocals, percussion
Steve Morse: guitars, vocals
Don Airey: keyboards
Roger Glover: bass, keyboards, vocals, percussion
Ian Paice: drums and percussion
Bob Ezrin: backing vocals
Nicole Thalia: backing vocals
Marsha B. Morrison: backing vocals
Leo Green: tenor saxophone
Matt Holland: trumpet
Gina Forsyth: fiddle
Bruce Diagrepont: squeezebox
Julian Shank: percussion
Record label: earMUSIC
Recorded at The Tracking Room, Nashville, US; Real World Studios, Wiltshire, UK, in 2020
Produced by Bob Ezrin
Release date: 26 November 2021
Highest chart places: UK: 28, US: did not chart
Running time: 49:45

Album Facts

Soon after the release of *Whoosh!,* the COVID pandemic hit. This forced the usually hard-working band to stay home, but *Whoosh!*'s success rekindled everyone's enthusiasm for recording. They tried jamming (and writing) via Zoom, but the results were unsatisfying. So, the group decided to do a covers album instead.

Although the band had covered other artists' songs before ('Hush', 'Kentucky Woman', 'Help', 'We Can Work It Out' and most recently 'Roadhouse Blues' on *InFinite*), this is the first time they would do an album entirely of other artists' songs. They may also have been encouraged by the fact that only a few years before, The Rolling Stones had hit number one on the UK album chart with *Blue And Lonesome*, their first entirely non-original album.

Glover told *Forbes*' Jim Ryan in 2021 that they took a vote on which songs they wanted to record. Democratic it may have been, but none of Gillan's suggestions made the final cut, which had a broad palette of songs. While most choices date back to the band members' younger days, that doesn't necessarily mean that these were songs that heavily influenced them. Johnny Horton, for example, is about as far removed from 'Fireball' as Mantovani from the Sex Pistols.

Album choices decided, they had to overcome the fact that the band members were never able to be in the same room at the same time. Glover told Ryan that Ezrin devised a method that involved recording the basic tracks in members' own homes.

> ...which kind of went into a pool in Nashville governed by Bob Ezrin, and he farmed it out to all the people who needed to put solos on, or this, that, and the other.

There was one exception to the solo work. Glover flew to England to work on the vocals with Gillan, and these were recorded in just four days. These vocal tracks were sent to Nashville and added to the instruments before the final mixing. Given the circumstances, the whole process from concept to package was surprisingly quick and *Turning To Crime* was released only a year after its predecessor. No two DP studio albums since *Burn* and *Stormbringer* in 1974 had been released this closely together.

The album name came about after Gillan suggested, tongue-in-cheek, that some would consider it a crime for DP to do covers. The band were so taken by this that *Turning To Crime* was taken on as the album's moniker.

However, the album would slow the band's recent chart momentum, reaching no higher than 15 on the UK album charts and not featuring at all in the US *Billboard* top 100, although like its two predecessors, it would reach number one in both the UK's Independent album and the Rock and Metal albums charts.

Album Cover

After the favourable reaction to their cover for *Whoosh!*, Milan-based graphic designers Jekyll & Hyde were asked back to handle this project, which could not have been more different from its predecessor while being just as busy. The *Turning To Crime* cover proves that DP has come a long way in the nearly 40 years since the reunion. Back in 1984, the cover designers for *Perfect Strangers* did their utmost to play down the age of the band by keeping their faces off the front and manipulating their photos on the back. What we have here is the opposite. In recent photoshoots, the band has tried to look at least a little funky. Here, the photos show all the band members looking their worst. The hair is wild, and the expressions are very old-man, perhaps grandfatherish. Gillan told Italian radio that the idea came after he had an unfortunate photo taken on a windy day:

> I looked like an escaped convict. So, I showed the photograph to the office, and they all said: 'If we do that with everyone, they will look like mugshots.'

The result is exactly that: a series of unforgiving black & whites that could not be less rock god. They each hold a police identification slate with their name and place of abode drawn in various fonts. Their expressions are as cross as if you had done a crayon drawing on their hall wall. Sorry, grandad.

Morse told the author the shots were an attempt to look authentic but quickly added that 'the band does have a sense of humour'.

The rest of the cover is equally grungy. Images of sticky tape and a paperclip hold the photos, and the old type print, as in a police charge sheet, tells us the name of the album and, on the back, the production credits. Also on the back is a pre-computer edit of the track list, with whole lines blanked out, as, again, in a court document.

It also fits with the nature of the album, which involves them playing songs that are equally as aged but were young and fresh when they were young and fresh. It is a wonderfully irreverent cover concept, fine in execution, and notably, the first time DP members have been on their own studio album front cover since *Come Taste The Band* in 1975. Good on them for daring to be brave. And Mr Morse is right. It is funny.

'7 And 7 Is' (Arthur Lee)

Written by Arthur Lee and released on his band Love's 1966 album *Da Capo,* this is a track that has a lot in common with the early DP. Fast and heated in its original form, it found a market among rebellious youth, reaching 33 on the *Billboard* Pop chart. The DP version is remarkably similar with extremely fast 16th note drumming, but there are a few differences: the original's twang guitar was reinterpreted nicely by Airey and Morse, and there's an organ solo instead of the half-time ending. Paice works his drums hard here, including short triplet sections at 1.39 and 2.14.

This is a piece that forgives no lapse of concentration. The result is that the new version blasts from the beginning, stays that way for most of the journey and then finishes suddenly. A fine accomplishment and a solid way to begin the album. That the band was this tight despite recording their parts in separate countries is astonishing.

'Rockin' Pneumonia And The Boogie Boogie Flu' (Huey 'Piano' Smith)

This was a 1957 top 100 *Billboard* charter for Huey Smith and then recorded by many people, including Professor Longhair in 1974. The Smith version was a slow, sexy, swaying number, but DP's version owes more to the Longhair reinterpretation. A big difference between that release and this is that the Professor didn't stretch out nearly as much as Gillan, who has turned the track into a more urgent thing. It's Airey, though, who makes the most of it. His piano dances all over this song, with glissandos and even a 'Smoke On The Water' motif thrown in. The choice to do this at the faster pace skates it along, but it would have been fascinating to see the band do it in Smith's slower style. That might have really been something.

'Oh Well' (Peter Green)

This 1969 Fleetwood Mac single was a guitarist's delight with its contrasts between a frantic and a slow, almost bolero, style. Morse apes the Mac's guitar opening before he multi-tracks himself. This works well in the DP format with the keyboard and guitar solos, which are far wilder than the original. The drums are also a part of the 2020 technology, which adds a monstrous tom depth. The quiet section remains, but the dinky cowbell of the original is well replaced by snare rimshots. Gillan is so exuberant that it's almost as if he's back in the playful 1970s, and this playfulness extends to the music video, directed by Dan Gibling, where The Purps are a masked gang that robs a younger band of their instruments before chasing a young Bob Dylan down a road in their 1960s getaway van and stealing his songbook. The police swoop and the band members are shown having their mugshots taken. It is a compelling piece of video art that shows a surprising amount of authenticity for a group that has never been known for its acting skills, but they do just fine here.

'Jenny Take A Ride' (Bob Crewe)
This album highlight, co-written by The Four Seasons' songwriter and producer, hit number one on the US R&B charts for Mitch Ryder and The Detroit Wheels in 1965. The first part of the song, the 'See See Rider' refrain, was later adopted by Elvis Presley for the opening medley of his live shows. More recently, it was used in the soundtrack for the movie *Once Upon A Time In Hollywood*, which may have brought it to the band's attention. This high-energy adaptation is full of interesting twists and turns, for example, Glover's uncharacteristic walking bass line. Airey gives a piano solo of several parts while Gillan moves through the octaves with the sort of confidence he threw into 'New Orleans' with the Gillan band 40 years before. With this kind of verve on show, one could almost think they do better away from each other. Almost.

'Watching The River Flow' (Bob Dylan)
Bob Dylan wrote and recorded this shuffle blues in 1971 as an upbeat number which reads as an indictment of human behaviour. Dylan's track was dominated by a bopping piano, courtesy of producer Leon Russell. It's easy to see what DP found attractive about it, so it is some surprise then that they changed it into a straight rocker. There is still a shuffle feel, but Airey is much further down in the mix than Russell. When he gets a chance to solo, it is with his Hammond, not piano, which changes the feel of the track considerably. By heavying the song, DP swamps the Dylan track's intrinsic humour, making this one of the few songs on the album where the original far outshines the cover.

'Let The Good Times Roll' (Sam Theard, Fleecie Moore)
Things get back on track with this saucy blues, which was first recorded by Louis Jordan and his Tympany Five in 1946. It's a smart song with clever lyrics, and in 1946, it must have been about as sexy as a five-piece band could

get. And DP keep it slow and swanky. Paice especially seems to be enjoying himself the most here, with his jazz chops to the fore. Glover plays a fuzzy walking bass and Airey throws four or five styles into the mix. Gillan hasn't been noted as a singer of early blues, but he does the job well here, although he can't resist a Gillan scream at the end. Morse does a cool, slow guitar solo that harks back to some of his Dixie Dregs work. In all, this track proves Paice's belief that DP is a swinging rock band.

'Dixie Chicken' (Lowell George, Fred Martin)
The eponymous track from Little Feat's 1973 *Dixie Chicken* album is a New Orleans funk-style cruiser. The track would seem a good match for DP, being a piano and guitar song with an overdose of humour. The opening here is quite different from the original drum groove, with Paice offering a more martial set of snare rudiments before setting a solid New Orleans beat. The guitar and piano pay homage to Little Feat's interpretation, with Morse especially cutting loose and flitting between genres. The song is made for Gillan's storytelling style, and he doesn't disappoint.

'Shapes Of Things' (Jim McCarty, Keith Relf, Paul Samwell-Smith)
One of the few outright pop songs on the album, it was written by young men wondering about their futures, so it might seem odd it is then that the mature men of DP should choose to cover it. It is likely that the environmental theme was the attraction, along with its slightly psychedelic nature. DP don't change the monster hook that in 1966 gave The Yardbirds a number three in the UK. Ezrin does choose to give the song a 1960s sound, which is occasionally very close to the original, as is Gillan's vocal, at times matching Keith Relf's tone, although he breaks out of the mimicry a few times by sliding between notes. DP handle the song's snappy changes with aplomb, injecting just enough new vibe, most notably with the guitar solo, which is unmistakably more Steve Morse than Jeff Beck. The organ solo near the end is also definitely DP.

'The Battle Of New Orleans' (Jimmy Driftwood)
As if there weren't enough of a genre mix on this album, the band decides to attack this country and western-style war song best known for Johnny Horton's humorous 1959 take. Writer Jimmy Driftwood released his own version in 1936, which bore little resemblance to Horton's more military interpretation. And it is the Horton version that DP revisit, perhaps because the song has a history with the DP alumni. Gillan and Glover's previous band, Episode Six, used to perform it, with Glover singing. Glover is the main singer here this time, too, and joined after the first verse by Gillan, Morse, and Ezrin. Bruce Daigrepont's squeeze box and Gin Forsyth's fiddle are the lead instruments, although Morse manages to squeeze in a few guitar lines here and there. It's fun but a truly odd inclusion on the album. And about as DP as, well, Johnny Horton.

'Lucifer' (Bob Seger)
This 1970 track from Bob Seger's *Mongrel* album has a verve, but Gillan transforms it out of its grungy original style. Truer are bassline and keyboards, although about halfway through, Airey succumbs to the desire to put his own stamp on it. Yes, there were a few rushes of blood to the head here. This version might have been better without them.

'White Room' (Jack Bruce, Pete Brown)
The sound of Cream's masterpiece is so much in the public consciousness that any attempt to cover it on record carries the risk of comparison. In this case, the opening is a mirror image of the 1968 single, but it offers all the power that modern studios can offer, including Paice's opening fusillade. Morse's guitars are everywhere and cut through more than Eric Clapton's. In fact, Cream's quite thin tone is filled out, especially by a wall of keyboards from Airey. So, there's a lot going on here (five DP members versus Cream's three, plus viola, perhaps), but it works. Gillan's voice is obviously the biggest point of difference. Jack Bruce's was clean and simple and his highs clear. Gillan achieves the range with the help of overdubbing, but it sounds less convincing. Morse has reserved his best solo for this track (and after all, he is stepping into Clapton territory), and as a revisit, he does himself and DP proud. The fadeout at what seems to be mid-solo sounds odd, just as it was on the original.

'Caught In The Act'
The album ends with a mostly instrumental medley that is equally as eclectic as the tracks on the rest of the album. The difference with a medley is that its songs need to move into each other effectively. The Beatles managed to do it with a group of disparate Lennon and McCartney musical waifs on the second side of *Abbey Road*. Here, DP try a similar feat. The songs here are strong, but the result is no *Abbey Road*.

(a) 'Going Down' (Don Nix)
The medley starts with this Airey showcase with the repeated line 'down down'. Tight throughout, it stops suddenly, giving 'Green Onions' a chance to open cleanly.

(b) 'Green Onions' (Booker T. Jones, Steve Cropper, Lewis Steinberg, Al Jackson Jr)
Morse dominates this track as a contrast to Airey's true-to-the-Booker organ. Booker T and the MGs were never this heavy, and as a result, this does have plenty of DP DNA all over it, maybe a little too much. While Paice and Glover provide a rhythm section that grooves appropriately, Morse does a solo that breaks out from the laid-back vibe and probably doesn't need to.

(c) 'Hot 'Lanta' (Duane Allman, Gregg Allman, Dickey Betts, Butch Trucks, Berry Oakley, Jai Johanny Johnson)
A seamless segue leads into this 1971 Allman Brothers Band live staple. Hot and frantic, it matches the original Fillmore East recording for intensity, except for Paice, who, for once, doesn't try to play all Butch Trucks' notes.

(d) 'Dazed And Confused' (Jake Holmes, Jimmy Page, Robert Plant)
An interesting, fast intro leads into Led Zeppelin's version of Jake Holmes' dirty blues. Where Zeppelin made the most of the song, DP doesn't. This is, unfortunately, way too short, impatient to lead into The Spencer Davis Group's 1966 hit.

(e) 'Gimme Some Lovin'' (Steve Winwood, Spencer Davis, Muff Linwood)
'Gimme Some Lovin' is the only track on the medley where Gillan gets a vocal. DP gives an enthusiastic stab at it, but Gillan seems inexplicably laid back. It's a good listen, but perhaps a purely instrumental version or a higher key might have been a little more exciting as an album end note, particularly as there was a chance, at the time, that this might be the last DP track.

= 1 (2024)

Personnel
Ian Gillan: vocals
Roger Glover: bass
Ian Paice: drums and percussion
Don Airey: keyboards
Simon McBride: guitars
Bob Ezrin: backing vocals, percussion
Patricia Shirley-Okujene: backing vocals
Camille Harrison: backing vocals
Record label: earMUSIC
Recorded at Ocean Way, Nashville, US; Noble Street, Toronto, Canada; Headline, Harston, UK; SMB Chameleon, Hamburg, Germany, 2023 and 2024
Produced by Bob Ezrin
Release date: 19 July 2024
Highest chart places: UK: 6, US: did not chart
Running time: 52.06

Album Facts

When the COVID-delayed *Whoosh!* tour finally got underway in late 2022, it was without Morse, the guitarist having told the band he needed time off touring so he could tend to his seriously ill wife. Morse's temporary replacement for the tour was suggested by Airey: Simon McBride, who had been in Sweet Savage, Snakecharmer and Airey's own solo band. A few months later, it was reported that Morse had decided to leave the band permanently and that McBride had been asked to stay as his replacement. So sudden was the change that the tour publicity still had Morse's image on it.

Morse told the author that he intended to rejoin the band, but after he asked for another year off, the band refused. Glover told *Classic Rock*'s Dave Everley in August 2024 that it was, in essence, a firing:

> He got [the news that he was being let go] from the management, but I called him and we talked. He was not happy, either. It was hard and sad, and after 28 years of making some great music with Steve, it was... for me, it was a tough decision. But that's life sometimes.

Gillan told *Classic Rock*'s Fraser Lewry in 2022 that age was one factor in that decision:

> As we get older, we realise that we're much closer to the end, and that triggers an urgency that won't be tamed. From Steve's perspective, I can only imagine that there is no possible 'nice' way of continuing with a new man, but it is either that or call it a day because the lack of momentum was gradually becoming something more significant; it felt terminal.

Morse told the author that personal trauma aside, the time was probably right to part ways:

> Having left and looking back on how hungry I was to get back to being a major contributor to the direction of the bands I'm in, I think, yeah, it was definitely time, and I think they're much happier with the very high-quality work that Simon is doing.

And they were happy. In July 2024, Glover told *Billboard*'s Gary Graff that it was McBride's live performances with the band that got them enthused to do another original album. The enthusiasm was helped by good news on the record sales front. The Super Deluxe Edition *Machine Head,* with remixes by Dweezil Zappa, had reached number 30 in the UK.

In April 2023, the band started recording new material, and Bob Ezrin produced it for the fifth time. One year later, the band released their first original single in four years; two others quickly followed, and the new album was released on 19 July. The marketing began well in advance, with white billboards with arithmetic equations popping up in European capitals. Full-page ads in major music magazines also testified to the label's belief in the product. Much of this publicity and promo work involved takes on the album title *=1*, a title that continued the enigmatic nature of their post-Blackmore release names. The band's own website tries to explain the intent of the moniker:

> '=1' symbolises the idea that in a world growing ever more complex, everything eventually simplifies down to a single, unified essence. Everything equals one.

And the album does show a band in unison, although there's no mistaking the difference between McBride and Morse: where Morse's chugging riffs and screaming high notes were his totems, McBride's down-and-dirty riffing is more guitar-hero. McBride's persona onstage is also very different. McBride wears a serious, concentrated look for much of the show, like Blackmore, while Morse, even after 25 years, was an ever-smiling presence, looking like he was loving every second of it (Morse told the author that he wasn't acting).

In 2024, Gillan would tell *This Is Rock*'s Tony Gonzales that the change of guitarists was a revelation:

> Simon is a genius. He's got all the energy and articulation and musical skills and creative skills that you could ever dream of. It's one of the best things that could have happened to the band.

One thing that would not change with the new member was the studio method. McBride revealed on the official DP website that the recording process remained in the Ezrin style: fast with a minimum of wastage:

> Many of the songs, like 'Portable Door', were written in the first sessions and literally came together in 5 or 10 minutes. It all was so easy and natural. And the album feels that way, too.

The remarkable thing about this album is Gillan. His voice is almost indistinguishable from that on *Perfect Strangers*. His ability to slide ever so easily up and down a scale is all over the album. The rest of the band are also revelling, with Glover and Paice sounding their most liberated for a long time. It's a set of delicate five-way performances that feel early-1970s DP while being, for the most part, new. It's a trip and a satisfying one.

Critics felt the same way. *Classic Rock* magazine's John Aizlewood gave the album nine out of ten. A big call, but one that the fans obviously agreed with. In the US, *=1* reached number 19 on the rock album chart, which is DP's best album result since *Perfect Strangers* 40 years before. It also went to number six in the UK and number one in Germany, Sweden and Switzerland, sending *=1* into rarified air as a worldwide chart success for the band.

Album Cover

This minimalist cover is as simple as *Whoosh!* was busy. Not dissimilar to the *Now What?!* design, we have a white cover with the band name in a capitalised cursive font in the middle with the album title just above. The back cover has the songs' names unnumbered and separated only by commas, with the producer credit underneath. Strangely, the CD packaging pays homage to *Whoosh!,* with each CD having what appears to be a series of planets and nebulae, which may be the perspective of looking out from inside a black hole. The planets are also in the booklets, which are otherwise spartan with typeface lyrics, credits and a couple of geometric figures. The vinyl albums have no such astronomical references, with centre labels similar to the cover artwork and the vinyl itself in purple. The rest of the packaging is as elaborate as the cover is simple, with a 16-page booklet and bonus live tracks. Gatefold vinyl editions have the vinyl itself in various colours, and there are box sets with lots of merchandise, dual CDs, gatefold LPs and even cassettes. EarMUSIC was determined to package this release as an event and did so, covering every single base.

All tracks by Gillan, Glover, Paice, Airey, McBride, Ezrin (unless otherwise noted)

'Show Me'

And this is what we get from the new guy: McBride stamps himself from the very beginning with a fingertip razz layered with his own answering run. It quickly develops into a song of many quickfire parts and turns: scats are interspersed with choruses, bridges, descensions, middle-eights and rappish interludes in the style of 'Any Fule Kno That'. Gillan is in great form, beginning by panting before going straight into the changes with real energy. The song has plenty of lyrical defiance, at one point, telling the listener, 'We're not going anywhere'. Obviously.

It's an exhilarating piece of work and full of life. More importantly, it's new and, as such, a perfect opener for a new-era album.

'A Bit On The Side'

This is guitar-hero stuff. Dirtier in sound than even Blackmore, but still with that guitarist's riffing sensibility, this is the kind of work that has been done many times by hard rock bands from Kiss to Metallica. Like riff songs, it is not about the whole band as such. Airey has little to do for the first half but gets a solo, along with, briefly, Paice. They all feel slightly obligatory. That can't be said of McBride's late solo, which cracks along, as does Glover's constant 16th-note thrum under the guitarist.

It seems at first that Gillan is not going to stretch himself as he did on the first track. He is happy to just tell his story, and he does it in the second person, talking to Charlene, who has arrived from the country and embeds herself in a seedy city. She makes a pass at the singer, who responds by pointing the moral finger before becoming more understanding:

> You may not be much different to me
> You got to earn a living
> With the tools that you were given

Thirty years ago, Gillan and Glover's lyrics had no such reflection. These ones have depth, and the song is better for it, lifting it out of what really is just a beautifully executed rock grunge.

'Sharp Shooter'

The heaviness gets heavier. McBride is starting to sound more and more like two guitars, or is it that Airey is now in full guitar-mirror mode? Solos flow into each other, each as a kind of prelude to the one that follows. It's as if the band has consciously said it won't be bound by this verse/chorus/solo/chorus straitjacket. After the interesting opening, the song eases slightly off the pedal for the verses.

The lyrics are in the singer's criticism genre. Yet Gillan is not the titular sharpshooter but the sharp shooter's target. Gillan is defiant. Others, he sings, have taken aim at him before, but he is still here. It's hard to go past the interpretation that the lyrics are aimed at critics, but the violence and implied threat in the words make it sound as if he's playing a role in *High Noon*. The words, tough as they are, are a perfect complement to the anger in the music. This may prove to be a favourite for fans of DP's heaviest work, but for others, the busyness might be just too thick for real engagement. There's also an odd feeling that the band has done this before.

'Portable Door'

The first single from the album and their first recording with McBride indicates that with Morse gone, things are not going to be radically different. The guitars and the synths still mirror each other for much of the song and the bass and drums maintain a solid undercurrent. The music also carries a similar feel to some tracks from earlier albums, particularly 'Throw My Bones' from *Whoosh!* and 'Time For Bedlam' from *InFinite* (Gillan and Airey at times almost repeat the motif and cadence of that track) and going back even further there are tones of 'Pictures Of Home'. It's lively, though, and Gillan is in great voice, particularly in the choruses when he goes into some fine higher register work. McBride gives the song its thrust, particularly in his solo. This track is also notable for Paice's snare/bass drum syncopation. It's only on close listening that you realise that this great shuffler has never done this kind of '60s syncopation on a DP song before. And he does it very well.

After all the political, environmental and social messaging of latter DP albums, this is a return to Gillan's obtuse storytelling, not dissimilar to his wonderful rant in 'Somebody Stole My Guitar' from *Purpendicular*, but this is more about conversation and philosophy. Gillan told *Mojo*'s Mark Blake that the title originated from a quirky thought:

> Wouldn't it be handy to carry a portable door around, then you could slip in and out of situations whenever you wanted…

If you're going to reboot a band, this is just the sort of wacko concept that might do the trick.

The song's video by Leo Feimer is the first for the new lineup and is surprisingly small, with the band shown close together, performing the song without spacemen, ferals or backstage hijinks. Gillan gives the camera some meaningfully dark glances while the rest of the band just... plays. The cool award goes to hatted and maroon-jacketed Glover, the only band member who looks like he's given more than two minutes thought to the dress code. In all, it is a lively song that has the characteristic DP verve, but no particularly new ground has been broken in either the song or its video.

'Old-Fangled Thing'

A variation in pace, heaviness and style, this is a corker. McBride, Airey and Paice snap out an exquisite and exciting 20-second opening until Gillan enters with another storybook lyric. We've heard his story before: he is drinking, he has his guitar, and he is met by the 'you'. Even Gillan admits that it all sounds familiar, but just when you think we're headed into his stolen guitar/night of sex territory, Gillan changes tack, poking fun at himself (listen for the reference to a 'living wreck').

Gillan's lyric is ostensibly about the invention of the pencil, of all things, but he turns this modest premise into a work of double entendre, the boldest since 'Knocking At Your Back Door':

Why does your eraser have a handle so long?
It's for the lead in my pencil man, I got to keep it sharp
Knock it into shape, I can't go wrong
But even then... when I'm done... here comes another part

He's having fun, and so is the band. Airey does lovely fingertip play in short bursts, which adds to the surprise. Likewise, Paice puts in half-bars of jazz fusion. Halfway through, the song turns with some lovely guitar-led angst, abetted by some fabulous Glover bass work.

All this results in an odd album highlight. If there is a drawback to this song, it is that it shows just how samey other songs in the catalogue can sound.

'If I Were You'

Then, we have a big change of pace in the monster ballad genre. Over the years, the reunion DP has done this with mixed success, from 'Love Conquers All' to 'Wasted Sunsets'. This one, though, starts promisingly. McBride's guitar, particularly his superb solo, has some evocative tones of Morse's work on the *Bananas* ballad 'Haunted'.

More than 20 years on from that marginal song, Gillan gives us something more successful, an emotive plea that uses his range cleanly. The lyrics talk of a betrayal, but love isn't mentioned. It's about a best friend who did him wrong many years ago. One obvious interpretation is that it is directed at Glover or Paice, who were involved in the decision to fire Gillan back in the 1980s. This would be odd because Paice told Friedlander this was one of his album favourites. It would also be odd because so much water has passed under that bridge that it would be particularly sad if Gillan was still bearing a grudge 35 years later. It is most probable that he is inventing, using the emotion of that time as just one element in making the lyric authentic. And his delivery is certainly that. Gillan doesn't sound like he is acting, and frankly, the rest of the band keeps out of his way. They know what he is doing. McBride does allow himself a few too many flourishes, perhaps, but there is respect all around for a man just trying to tell a very personal story. The last minute is something special, with guitar and organ leading a refrain that gently underlines Gillan's lovely, repeated closing mantra.

'Pictures Of You'

This is another song that shows the difference between McBride and Morse. Opening with a couple of notes in a fashion similar to 'Into The Fire' from the early days, the song quickly changes into something funky and jolting.

McBride has somehow gone the full Blackmore here without actually copying Blackmore. He also gives a new sound towards the end that is daringly more ELO in tone. It's great to see that so early in his time with the band, he is going so broad.

The lyrics are a memory of someone, and in the situation of Gillan's own loss (his wife Bron died only a year or so earlier), one interpretation could be that this song is very personal. If so, joy still seeps through every line because the song also seems to be a celebration of the lost one, of this new band, of the new life it brings.

The words are delivered in an urgent voice with phrasing that both follows the melody (in the chorus) and slips into the gaps (in the verses and middle eight). Thus, musically and lyrically, the song is always interesting; even the very end, with its string synth outro, is something new, poignant and satisfying.

'I'm picking up a new vibe', sings Gillan.

Indeed.

'I'm Saying Nothin''

DP has often found difficulty in finding different ways to open their songs. They had no problems with this one, choosing to have Gillan belt right at the outset, backed with a guitar, bass and drum thump. From there, we tread more familiar ground, with echoes of the vocals of 'I've Got Your Number' and Morse's grind in 'Fingers To The Bone'. Paice told *American Songwriter*'s Matt Friedlander this is one of his favourites on the album:

> I think that harkens back to a couple of the tracks on the old *In Rock* record. It's got a sort of similar vibe, an incredibly simple but catchy little riff, and a nice lyric.

And it's true that the lyrics are an interesting follow-on from some of the semi-autobiographical soul-searching we've seen earlier on the album. This time, the singer promises not to reveal anything at all; he's keeping schtum, and ironically, he devotes a whole song to telling us this. It's not the most compelling of storylines because there really isn't one.

The singing also closely follows the guitar riff, and a contrast or an answer would have done this track a huge service. Despite Paice's high opinion, this lack of variation, the nothing lyrics and the one-dimensional groove let down the fascinating work that's going on elsewhere on the set.

'Lazy Sod'

After the autopilot of the last track, this is a killer piece of work. It's a heavy, mid-tempo blues with a strong hook. Once again, Gillan's voice belies the years. There's no strain, no apparent compromise. McBride's solo has a lot in common with that of Morse, with rave chugs and those occasional highs, and Airey gives us variations of his bouncy synth soloing before delivering a lovely ascension a minute from the end.

The story behind the title is rather prosaic, inspired by a journalist jokingly calling Gillan a lazy sod for only penning 500 songs (compared to Dolly Parton's 5000), but Gillan and Glover turn this unpromising start into something more; an extension of *Whoosh!*'s life extinction theme. There's climate change's smoke and rising waters, but this time, the singer can't be bothered, knowing there's nothing he can do about it. As such, it can be read as having the intent of 'Nothing At All', but writ small, and going further in recognition that his hopes have been defeated.

He is lazy, stays in bed, and worries about forgetting to turn the light off. And in a chutzpah moment, he tells the listener they can like it or not. Go, Gillan.

Just like in the first two singles, this one's music video just shows the band playing in a white set, but the difference here is the clever, fast cutting and odd angles, including an overhead shot of the keyboards that make them look like they go on forever. Gillan is shown full body, doing groovy dancing to the music. There are also a few cool moments where the band members morph into each other. A metaphorical statement of brotherhood, perhaps? The author watched the video on release with one of Australia's rising young rock singers, who said it was extremely cool. She got that right.

'Now You're Talkin''

The coolness extends to this fast piece, which starts with synth and guitar melding to give an opening effect of ... I don't know what, really. It's wacky in the tradition of the ventilator at the start of 'Fireball', and like on that track, it serves no purpose except to warn of the strong stuff to come. And it comes with a new interpretation of the fast straight rock style. Paice is at his most muscular with an extremely fast single bass drum.

What is most remarkable about this song is Gillan. It's wonderful to have the singer, for the second time on this album, challenging his range to the point of vocal shredding. He takes us back to his hedonistic days of free sex and might just be suggesting it's what the world needs a bit more of just now:

Whatever does you good
Lifts your skirt
Gets you done
Unbuttons your shirt
Wakes you up
Turns your head
Hits the spot
Now you're talkin'

Fittingly, his voice is eerily similar to his pre-reunion solo days with its playfulness and flirtiness. It's as if the earnest vocal proselytising and preaching of *Whoosh!* never happened. Nice to have Gillan's Gillan back.

'No Money To Burn'

Gillan continues in great voice on this blues-style number. Gillan's gushes about McBride are well justified on this track, not for his solo (which is very good, by the way), but for his stop/start riff, which is wrapped tight with Airey and Glover.

McBride might have that guitar hero aura about him, but he's no egotist. He understands the importance of space, and it's in McBride's spaces that Gillan struts his stuff. The subject matter may be in the old blues vein, with its complaints about life (in this case, about having no money), yet it's upbeat, as so many of the old swamp blues were. It also suits Glover, who gives gorgeous bass runs under Airey's solo. In all, this is a track that will probably be on a listener's high rotation. It's that cool, honest and energising.

'I'll Catch You'

If the previous track took us to the days of classic blues roots, this one goes back but to an entirely different era, the Jeff Beck '70s style, where guitars ruled in minor keys. DP has been there before, of course, on 'Wasted Sunsets', and like that track, this tries a bit too hard to touch the listeners' emotions. McBride begins in that Beck style and then drops down as Gillan emotes in the second-person to a lover with lyrics too convoluted for the honesty of the singing:

I have to keep a straight face
When I'm breaking up inside
If you know who, knew what I thought
Then we'd both be crucified

This busyness is unfortunate because Gillan is again in great vocal form and McBride's solo is astounding. Airey's strong synths are emotional compasses, highlighting the sadness of the piece. The ending is a beauty, adding memorable weight to Gillan's simple last lines:

I'll catch you in my arms
Anytime, anytime, anytime you want to jump
I'll catch you in my arms

If the honesty here had played through the whole song, it could have been a classic. What we have instead is a highly wrought piece that doesn't quite touch despite superb playing from all concerned.

'Bleeding Obvious'

This, the final album track, could be what DP has always stood for: progressive power music. Glover also says it took a lot of work to get right. One can see why. There are influences on display from all over the shop, referencing many eras of the band right through from 1968 (including a small snatch of guitar work that has a memory of DP's own 'Rat Bat Blue'). McBride and Airey lead in a series of sharp all-band hits that have the majesty of 'Perfect Strangers' but with the speed of the band's hard rock openers. That's quite a feat. And that's only the first half. A soft minute's work follows, where the theme of the album is revealed:

> If you ever return
> We'll see if you learned
> That it all adds up to one

Elsewhere in the lyrics, there are smatterings of references to the end of the road:

> Time is slipping by you know and things are moving fast
> You've got a long wait ahead my friend, if you save the best for last

The inference might seem obvious, but it could mean the opposite: there's more to come. Gillan and co. have been questioned for 20 years about the end of the band. It's entirely appropriate that they end the album with an enigma.

It's also proper that they end it with this album's statement: we're a unit and we are not teetering off into the sunset. And if this is their last original recording, they've left their fans well served.

Postscript

As several of the band members approach 80 years of age, they are fit, play with as much virtuosity as ever, and are still writing and touring. They also all look thrilled to be onstage. Their latest live journey follows on from *The Long Goodbye Tour* by being called the *=1 MORE TIME Tour*, tying in with the name of the latest studio album. The tour consisted of 60 concerts in Europe, the UK and the US.

One can only wonder about the next step for Gillan and Co. Certainly, McBride's recruitment has meant yet another regeneration after more than 55 years of regenerations, so much so that, as Gillan told *Mojo*'s Mark Blake in August 2024, the guitarist has the band members interacting again on a personal level. With this new mojo, there's every chance the latest tour will not be their last. One would not be wise to bet against further studio recordings, either.

This leaves us with what Ian Paice told *Rhythm* magazine in 2004 in answer to yet another retirement question:

> There are no Zimmer frames on stage yet.

Twenty years on, they still haven't appeared. The Roundabout continues.

Bibliography

Aizlewood, J., *The Hard Stuff, Albums: Deep Purple* (*Classic Rock*, Issue 329, p72)

Barton, G., *Jon Lord* (*Kerrang!* No 81, 15 – 28 November 1984)

Barton, G., *Ritchie Blackmore & Roger Glover* (Kerrang! No 82 29 November – 12 December 1984)

Beaver County Times, *Steve Morse On His Departure From Deep Purple* (17 May 2023)

Blabbermouth, *Joe Lynn Turner Finally Has True Love In His Life* (23 July 2007)

Blake, M., *Ian Gillan* (*Mojo*, August 2024)

Bloom, J., *More Black Than Purple* (Wymer Publishing, London, 2007).

Budofski, A., *Deep Purple's Ian Paice: Playing With Abandon* (*Modern Drummer*, December 1998)

Grow, K., *Deep Purple Plan 21st Album, 'Whoosh!'* (*Rolling Stone*, 17 March 2020)

Cashmere, P., *Deep Purple, the Whoosh! story and more* (Noise11.com, 23 August 2020)

Croatia television., *Gillan's Interview from Vienna '96* (The Highway Star, 3 April 1996)

Doerschuk, R., *Jurassic Rock* (*Keyboard Magazine*, January 1994)

Everley, D., *Ian Paice + Ian Gillan + Roger Glove +, Don Airey + Simon McBride = Deep Purple Mk IX* (Classic Rock, 330, August 2024)

Fessier, B., *Deep Purple's Don Airey Talks Evolving Sound, Indio Gig* (The Desert Sun, 12 August 2015)

Foster, M., *Deep Purple* (The Austrian Fan Mag, 1996)

Friedlander, M., *Deep Purple Drummer Ian Paice Talks the Concept Behind the New Album =1, Reveals His Favourite Songs From The New Record* (*American Songwriter*, 19 July 2024)

Gillan, I., *Ian Gillan. The Autobiography Of Deep Purple's Singer.* (Music Press Books, 1998)

Gillan, I., Interview at Fraser Island. *Total Abandon. Australia '99.* DVD. (Thompson Thames, 1999)

Gillan, I., *The ICD Annual Conference on Cultural Diplomacy 2012.* (The Institute for Cultural Diplomacy, Berlin, 13-16 December, 2012)

Glover, R., *Roger Glover & Bob Ezrin In Conversation* (Purple Maniac, earMUSIC, November 2019)

Gonzales, T., *Exclusive Interview with Ian Gillan of Deep Purple So Great* (This is Rock, 24 May 2024)

Graff, G., *Deep Purple On Upcoming Tour With Yes, Partying at Alice Cooper's 75th Birthday And New Album: 'We Can't Stop'* (*Billboard*, 18 July 2024)

Graham, J., *"I was playing the wrong key and everything, but it didn't seem to matter": Watch George Harrison play a Little Richard classic with Deep Purple in 1984* (*Guitar Player*, 6 December 2023)

Gruber, C., *Ian Paice Interview, Deep Purple: "I really didn't want to be doing anything else..."* (Everyone Loves Guitar, 9 October 2020)
Hart, C., *A Hart's Life* (Wymer, London, 2012)
Heide, R., *Change Is Life* (The Highway Star, 30 November 2003)
Herkkola, A., *Deep Purple Fan interview – Whoosh! Mission Crew – Episode 1.* (earMUSIC. 3 December 2020)
Hughes, A., *Jolly Roger* (*Bass Guitar Magazine*, August 2018)
Kafcaloudes, P., *Jon Lord Interview.* (In Pictures DVD. Thames Thompson, 2002).
Kafcaloudes, P., *Steve Morse Interview* (ABC Radio Australia 2005)
Kafcaloudes, P., *Steve Morse Interview* (22 March 2024)
Kafcaloudes, P., *Colin Hart Interview* (19 March 2024)
Kafcaloudes, P., *Drew Thompson Interview* (21 February 2024)
Kafcaloudes, P., *Joe Lynn Turner Interview* (4 March 2024)
Karlsson, D., *Roger Glover and Steve Morse Interview* (DPWWW. 8 March 1996)
Kleidermacher, M., *Where's There's Smoke... There's Fire!* (*Guitar World*, February 1991)
Kucera, I., *Ian Gillan & Jon Lord* (Muzikus '98. June 1998)
Lach, S., *Deep Purple Drummer Ian Paice Suffers Stroke* (*Classic Rock*, 17 June 2016)
Lewry, F., *Steve Morse To Step Away From Deep Purple Permanently: Band Pay Tribute* (*Classic Rock*, 23 July 2022)
Ling, D., *The Master Speaks* (The Highway Star, January 1987)
Ling, D., *Digging Deep* (*Classic Rock*, May 2024)
Lord, J., *Biography: Jon Lord* (Jon Lord Official Website)
Maariv, *Ian Gillan* (Maariv newspaper, Tel Aviv, December 1994)
Nishimoto, R., *Interview With Deep Purple* (The Highway Star, 1995)
Paice, I., *Ian Paice Nails Apres Vous One Take!* (Ian Paice's Drumtribe, 9 November 2022)
Paice, I., *Deep Purple* (*Uncut* magazine, April 2017)
Prato, G., *Ian Gillan Of Deep Purple* (Songfacts, 3 August 2020)
Putterford, M., *The Truth about Mitzi Dupree* (*Kerrang!* No 137, 8 January 1987)
Q95 Indianapolis, *Ian Gillan and Roger Glover interview* (Bob and Tom Show, 17 May 1996)
Rees, P., *To Infinity And Beyond* (*Classic Rock,* April 2017)
Rees, P., *Roger Glover* (*Classic Rock,* June 2018)
Resnicoff, M., *Baroque On The Water – Steve Morse joins Deep Purple* (Guitar Player, March 1995)
Robinson, J., *Fire In The Sky* (*Uncut*, April 2017)
Ryan, J., *Roger Glover On New Deep Purple Album 'Turning To Crime'* (Forbes, *26* November 2021)
Schneider, W., *Music Isn't To Be Trifled With* (The Highway Star, February 2024)

Simmons, S., *Deep Purple Reunite for Sylvie Simmons* (*Sounds*, 3 November 1984)
Stout, A.K., *Steve Morse Interview* (Knight Rider Newspapers, 10 August 1998)
Sulpasso, U., *Interview with Ian Gillan (Deep Purple)* (Radio Rock 106.6. Rome, 26 April 2017)
Tengner, A., *Metal Magazine – Deep Purple Special* (Z-TV. Sweden, 16 November 1993)
Vance, T., *Deep Purple Interviews* (The Friday Rock Show, November 1984)
Welch, C., *Ian Paice: Still Smokin'* (*Rhythm Magazine*, November 1995)
Welch, C., *Purple and Proud* (*Rhythm Magazine*, March 2004)
Zeltwanger, T., *Joe Satriani – The Newcomer In Deep Purple Speaks* (Metalstar, #6/7, July 1994)

Also available from Sonicbond

On Track series
Allman Brothers Band – Andrew Wild 978-1-78952-252-5
Tori Amos – Lisa Torem 978-1-78952-142-9
Aphex Twin – Beau Waddell 978-1-78952-267-9
Asia – Peter Braidis 978-1-78952-099-6
Badfinger – Robert Day-Webb 978-1-878952-176-4
Barclay James Harvest – Keith and Monica Domone 978-1-78952-067-5
Beck – Arthur Lizie 978-1-78952-258-7
The Beatles – Andrew Wild 978-1-78952-009-5
The Beatles Solo 1969-1980 – Andrew Wild 978-1-78952-030-9
Blue Oyster Cult – Jacob Holm-Lupo 978-1-78952-007-1
Blur – Matt Bishop 978-178952-164-1
Marc Bolan and T.Rex – Peter Gallagher 978-1-78952-124-5
Kate Bush – Bill Thomas 978-1-78952-097-2
Camel – Hamish Kuzminski 978-1-78952-040-8
Captain Beefheart – Opher Goodwin 978-1-78952-235-8
Caravan – Andy Boot 978-1-78952-127-6
Cardiacs – Eric Benac 978-1-78952-131-3
Nick Cave and The Bad Seeds – Dominic Sanderson 978-1-78952-240-2
Eric Clapton Solo – Andrew Wild 978-1-78952-141-2
The Clash – Nick Assirati 978-1-78952-077-4
Elvis Costello and The Attractions – Georg Purvis 978-1-78952-129-0
Crosby, Stills and Nash – Andrew Wild 978-1-78952-039-2
Creedence Clearwater Revival – Tony Thompson 978-178952-237-2
The Damned – Morgan Brown 978-1-78952-136-8
Deep Purple and Rainbow 1968-79 – Steve Pilkington 978-1-78952-002-6
Dire Straits – Andrew Wild 978-1-78952-044-6
The Doors – Tony Thompson 978-1-78952-137-5
Dream Theater – Jordan Blum 978-1-78952-050-7
Eagles – John Van der Kiste 978-1-78952-260-0
Earth, Wind and Fire – Bud Wilkins 978-1-78952-272-3
Electric Light Orchestra – Barry Delve 978-1-78952-152-8
Emerson Lake and Palmer – Mike Goode 978-1-78952-000-2
Fairport Convention – Kevan Furbank 978-1-78952-051-4
Peter Gabriel – Graeme Scarfe 978-1-78952-138-2
Genesis – Stuart MacFarlane 978-1-78952-005-7
Gentle Giant – Gary Steel 978-1-78952-058-3
Gong – Kevan Furbank 978-1-78952-082-8
Green Day – William E. Spevack 978-1-78952-261-7
Hall and Oates – Ian Abrahams 978-1-78952-167-2
Hawkwind – Duncan Harris 978-1-78952-052-1
Peter Hammill – Richard Rees Jones 978-1-78952-163-4
Roy Harper – Opher Goodwin 978-1-78952-130-6
Jimi Hendrix – Emma Stott 978-1-78952-175-7
The Hollies – Andrew Darlington 978-1-78952-159-7
Horslips – Richard James 978-1-78952-263-1
The Human League and The Sheffield Scene – Andrew Darlington 978-1-78952-186-3
The Incredible String Band – Tim Moon 978-1-78952-107-8
Iron Maiden – Steve Pilkington 978-1-78952-061-3
Joe Jackson – Richard James 978-1-78952-189-4
Jefferson Airplane – Richard Butterworth 978-1-78952-143-6
Jethro Tull – Jordan Blum 978-1-78952-016-3
Elton John in the 1970s – Peter Kearns 978-1-78952-034-7
Billy Joel – Lisa Torem 978-1-78952-183-2
Judas Priest – John Tucker 978-1-78952-018-7
Kansas – Kevin Cummings 978-1-78952-057-6
The Kinks – Martin Hutchinson 978-1-78952-172-6
Korn – Matt Karpe 978-1-78952-153-5
Led Zeppelin – Steve Pilkington 978-1-78952-151-1
Level 42 – Matt Philips 978-1-78952-102-3
Little Feat – Georg Purvis - 978-1-78952-168-9
Aimee Mann – Jez Rowden 978-1-78952-036-1
Joni Mitchell – Peter Kearns 978-1-78952-081-1
The Moody Blues – Geoffrey Feakes 978-1-78952-042-2
Motorhead – Duncan Harris 978-1-78952-173-3
Nektar – Scott Meze – 978-1-78952-257-0
New Order – Dennis Remmer – 978-1-78952-249-5
Nightwish – Simon McMurdo – 978-1-78952-270-9
Laura Nyro – Philip Ward 978-1-78952-182-5
Mike Oldfield – Ryan Yard 978-1-78952-060-6
Opeth – Jordan Blum 978-1-78-952-166-5
Pearl Jam – Ben L. Connor 978-1-78952-188-7
Tom Petty – Richard James 978-1-78952-128-3
Pink Floyd – Richard Butterworth 978-1-78952-242-6
The Police – Pete Braidis 978-1-78952-158-0
Porcupine Tree – Nick Holmes 978-1-78952-144-3
Queen – Andrew Wild 978-1-78952-003-3
Radiohead – William Allen 978-1-78952-149-8
Rancid – Paul Matts 989-1-78952-187-0
Renaissance – David Detmer 978-1-78952-062-0
REO Speedwagon – Jim Romag 978-1-78952-262-4
The Rolling Stones 1963-80 – Steve Pilkington 978-1-78952-017-0
The Smiths and Morrissey – Tommy Gunnarsson 978-1-78952-140-5
Spirit – Rev. Keith A. Gordon – 978-1-78952- 248-8
Stackridge – Alan Draper 978-1-78952-232-7
Status Quo the Frantic Four Years – Richard James 978-1-78952-160-3
Steely Dan – Jez Rowden 978-1-78952-043-9
Steve Hackett – Geoffrey Feakes 978-1-78952-098-9
Tears For Fears – Paul Clark - 978-178952-238-9
Thin Lizzy – Graeme Stroud 978-1-78952-064-4
Tool – Matt Karpe 978-1-78952-234-1
Toto – Jacob Holm-Lupo 978-1-78952-019-4
U2 – Eoghan Lyng 978-1-78952-078-1
UFO – Richard James 978-1-78952-073-6
Van Der Graaf Generator – Dan Coffey 978-1-78952-031-6
Van Halen – Morgan Brown – 9781-78952-256-3
The Who – Geoffrey Feakes 978-1-78952-076-7
Roy Wood and the Move – James R Turner 978-1-78952-008-8
Yes – Stephen Lambe 978-1-78952-001-9
Frank Zappa 1966 to 1979 – Eric Benac

978-1-78952-033-0
Warren Zevon – Peter Gallagher 978-1-78952-170-2
10CC – Peter Kearns 978-1-78952-054-5

Decades Series
The Bee Gees in the 1960s – Andrew Mon Hughes et al 978-1-78952-148-1
The Bee Gees in the 1970s – Andrew Mon Hughes et al 978-1-78952-179-5
Black Sabbath in the 1970s – Chris Sutton 978-1-78952-171-9
Britpop – Peter Richard Adams and Matt Pooler 978-1-78952-169-6
Phil Collins in the 1980s – Andrew Wild 978-1-78952-185-6
Alice Cooper in the 1970s – Chris Sutton 978-1-78952-104-7
Alice Cooper in the 1980s – Chris Sutton 978-1-78952-259-4
Curved Air in the 1970s – Laura Shenton 978-1-78952-069-9
Donovan in the 1960s – Jeff Fitzgerald 978-1-78952-233-4
Bob Dylan in the 1980s – Don Klees 978-1-78952-157-3
Brian Eno in the 1970s – Gary Parsons 978-1-78952-239-6
Faith No More in the 1990s – Matt Karpe 978-1-78952-250-1
Fleetwood Mac in the 1970s – Andrew Wild 978-1-78952-105-4
Fleetwood Mac in the 1980s – Don Klees 978-178952-254-9
Focus in the 1970s – Stephen Lambe 978-1-78952-079-8
Free and Bad Company in the 1970s – John Van der Kiste 978-1-78952-178-8
Genesis in the 1970s – Bill Thomas 978178952-146-7
George Harrison in the 1970s – Eoghan Lyng 978-1-78952-174-0
Kiss in the 1970s – Peter Gallagher 978-1-78952-246-4
Manfred Mann's Earth Band in the 1970s – John Van der Kiste 978178952-243-3
Marillion in the 1980s – Nathaniel Webb 978-1-78952-065-1
Van Morrison in the 1970s – Peter Childs - 978-1-78952-241-9
Mott the Hoople and Ian Hunter in the 1970s – John Van der Kiste 978-1-78-952-162-7
Pink Floyd In The 1970s – Georg Purvis 978-1-78952-072-9
Suzi Quatro in the 1970s – Darren Johnson 978-1-78952-236-5
Queen in the 1970s – James Griffiths 978-1-78952-265-5
Roxy Music in the 1970s – Dave Thompson 978-1-78952-180-1
Slade in the 1970s – Darren Johnson 978-1-78952-268-6
Status Quo in the 1980s – Greg Harper 978-1-78952-244-0
Tangerine Dream in the 1970s – Stephen Palmer 978-1-78952-161-0
The Sweet in the 1970s – Darren Johnson 978-1-78952-139-9
Uriah Heep in the 1970s – Steve Pilkington 978-1-78952-103-0
Van der Graaf Generator in the 1970s – Steve Pilkington 978-1-78952-245-7
Rick Wakeman in the 1970s – Geoffrey Feakes 978-1-78952-264-8
Yes in the 1980s – Stephen Lambe with David Watkinson 978-1-78952-125-2

On Screen series
Carry On… – Stephen Lambe 978-1-78952-004-0
David Cronenberg – Patrick Chapman 978-1-78952-071-2
Doctor Who: The David Tennant Years – Jamie Hailstone 978-1-78952-066-8
James Bond – Andrew Wild 978-1-78952-010-1
Monty Python – Steve Pilkington 978-1-78952-047-7
Seinfeld Seasons 1 to 5 – Stephen Lambe 978-1-78952-012-5

Other Books
1967: A Year In Psychedelic Rock 978-1-78952-155-9
1970: A Year In Rock – John Van der Kiste 978-1-78952-147-4
1973: The Golden Year of Progressive Rock 978-1-78952-165-8
Babysitting A Band On The Rocks – G.D. Praetorius 978-1-78952-106-1
Eric Clapton Sessions – Andrew Wild 978-1-78952-177-1
Derek Taylor: For Your Radioactive Children – Andrew Darlington 978-1-78952-038-5
The Golden Road: The Recording History of The Grateful Dead – John Kilbride 978-1-78952-156-6
Iggy and The Stooges On Stage 1967-1974 – Per Nilsen 978-1-78952-101-6
Jon Anderson and the Warriors – the road to Yes – David Watkinson 978-1-78952-059-0
Magic: The David Paton Story – David Paton 978-1-78952-266-2
Misty: The Music of Johnny Mathis – Jakob Baekgaard 978-1-78952-247-1
Nu Metal: A Definitive Guide – Matt Karpe 978-1-78952-063-7
Tommy Bolin: In and Out of Deep Purple – Laura Shenton 978-1-78952-070-5
Maximum Darkness – Deke Leonard 978-1-78952-048-4
The Twang Dynasty – Deke Leonard 978-1-78952-049-1

and many more to come!

Would you like to write for Sonicbond Publishing?

At Sonicbond Publishing we are always on the look-out for authors, particularly for our two main series:

On Track. Mixing fact with in depth analysis, the On Track series examines the work of a particular musical artist or group. All genres are considered from easy listening and jazz to 60s soul to 90s pop, via rock and metal.

On Screen. This series looks at the world of film and television. Subjects considered include directors, actors and writers, as well as entire television and film series. As with the On Track series, we balance fact with analysis.

While professional writing experience would, of course, be an advantage the most important qualification is to have real enthusiasm and knowledge of your subject. First-time authors are welcomed, but the ability to write well in English is essential.

Sonicbond Publishing has distribution throughout Europe and North America, and all books are also published in E-book form. Authors will be paid a royalty based on sales of their book.

Further details are available from www.sonicbondpublishing.co.uk. To contact us, complete the contact form there or email info@sonicbondpublishing.co.uk